As one of the world's longest established and best-known travel brands, Thomas Cook are the experts in travel.

For more than 135 years our guidebooks have unlocked the secrets of destinations around the world, sharing with travellers a wealth of experience and a passion for travel.

Rely on Thomas Cook as your travelling companion on your next trip and benefit from our unique heritage.

Thomas Cook **traveller** guides

THE GAMBIA
Lindsay Bennett

D0180356

Written by Lindsay Bennett, updated by Lisa Voormeij
Original photography by Pete Bennett

Published by Thomas Cook Publishing
A division of Thomas Cook Tour Operations Limited
Company registration no. 3772199 England
The Thomas Cook Business Park, Unit 9, Coningsby Road,
Peterborough PE3 8SB, United Kingdom
Email: books@thomascook.com, Tel: +44 (0) 1733 416477
www.thomascookpublishing.com

Produced by Cambridge Publishing Management Limited
Burr Elm Court, Main Street, Caldecote CB23 7NU
www.cambridgepm.co.uk

ISBN: 978-1-84848-428-3

© 2007, 2009 Thomas Cook Publishing
This third edition © 2011
Text © Thomas Cook Publishing
Maps © Thomas Cook Publishing/PCGraphics (UK) Limited

Series Editor: Karen Beaulah
Production/DTP: Steven Collins

Printed and bound in Spain by GraphyCems

Cover photography © Daphne Ouwersloot/Alamy

Contents

Introduction

This tiny sliver of a country, cutting a rapier-like plunge into the heart of West Africa, is inextricably bound to the meandering course of the mighty River Gambia. On a continent riven with civil war, famine and social strife, The Gambia is a beacon; a land of relative plenty, of social cohesion and of harmony.

Each of the country's ethnic groups has contributed to a fascinating culture that sustains a population of over one million, from tribal elders to the youngest in the family. The fabric of society is cemented by rites and rituals governing all aspects of life, offering the visitor a window into a totally different world.

Gambians are known for their friendliness; it's easy to see why the brochures call it 'The Smiling Coast'. There's a genuine *joie de vivre* here despite the fact that many live in poverty. It's apparent in the giggling children and the exuberant adults. Everyone here is curious to learn all about strangers in their midst – sometimes to the disquiet of more conservative foreigners.

So much about the country is an enigma, wrapped up in a puzzle, wrapped up in a conundrum. On the one hand The Gambia is a simple agrarian society, yet on the other it has one of the most vibrant and mature tourist industries on the continent. There are impassable roads, yet an international airport exists with a runway used as a backup by NASA should they have problems with bringing space shuttles down safely. It's what makes a visit so interesting; the more you see of the country, the less easy it is to pigeonhole it.

The Gambia has always sold itself as a winter sun destination, offering good value R&R in Western-style resorts with sandy beaches, swaying palms, swimming pools and a smiling waiter to deliver a cooling cocktail. And for visitors who simply want a relaxing holiday it certainly delivers, with an added touch of spice that's often missing in bland concrete Euro-resorts. The journey time from Western Europe is only six hours and The Gambia operates on GMT (the same time as the UK and Ireland and only one hour behind Central Europe), so no jet lag.

But as interest in ecotourism grows, the country seems destined to attract a whole new generation of fans. Much of the interior remains a pristine wilderness, a mixture of mangrove, savanna and deciduous forest that's home to important populations of plants and animals. It's already a top-rated destination for birdwatching and its reputation is bound to grow with the opening of several luxury lodges offering a range of quality sustainable experiences.

For travellers who have never visited sub-Saharan Africa before, The Gambia offers a gentle introduction to this most fascinating region. Here you've got the chance to test the waters of serious, dirt-in-your-boots, 'get away from it all' itineraries, but with the possibility of heading back to an air-conditioned hotel and a well-earned gin and tonic at the end of the day if you find the 'Mungo Park experience' (*see p107*) a little too much.

One trip could be the start of a whole new love affair.

A baobab tree laden with its fruit, known as 'monkey bread'

The land

The Republic of The Gambia is continental Africa's smallest country, but don't let its diminutive nature fool you into thinking the land has little to offer. The geography is more varied than that of many of its continental peers, with a wide range of natural ecosystems and a diverse array of flora and fauna to enjoy. The country has several internationally recognised protected areas, which stand it in good stead as interest in ecotourism grows.

The country

At 11,295sq km (4,361sq miles), The Gambia is just over half the size of Wales or slightly less than twice the size of the state of Delaware, but 1,300sq km (500sq miles) of this area is river, so the land mass is technically around 10,000sq km (4,000sq miles). The current borders were drawn up in 1889, agreed between the colonial powers Britain and France, giving the then British colony of Gambia a narrow stretch of territory on either bank of the river running 300km (186 miles) inland from the west coast of Africa. The country benefits from 80km (50 miles) of coastline but inland is only 48km (30 miles) wide at its fullest point; in the east, where the river is narrowest, this drops to around 15km (9 miles) wide – barely wide enough to register on maps of the continent. The 1889 agreement gave Gambia 740km (460 miles) of land borders, all of which are bounded by Senegal. In many ways the easiest explanation of the physical relationship between the two countries is that The Gambia is the meat layer in a Senegal sandwich.

The Gambia is a very flat land. The highest point in the country reaches only 53m (174ft) above sea level, though the river banks do include dramatic sand and laterite 'cliffs' which make impressive vantage points. Laterites are rocks with relatively high concentrations of iron and aluminium caused by the leaching effect of centuries of hard rain, and the resulting rock – a deep red-brown in colour – is used for bricks and, where asphalt is in short supply, for road surfaces.

The river

The River Gambia is one of Africa's great waterways. Rising some 1,130km (702 miles) inland in what is now the Republic of Guinea, the water journeys relentlessly westwards, crossing the border into The Gambia 480km (298 miles) from its mouth.

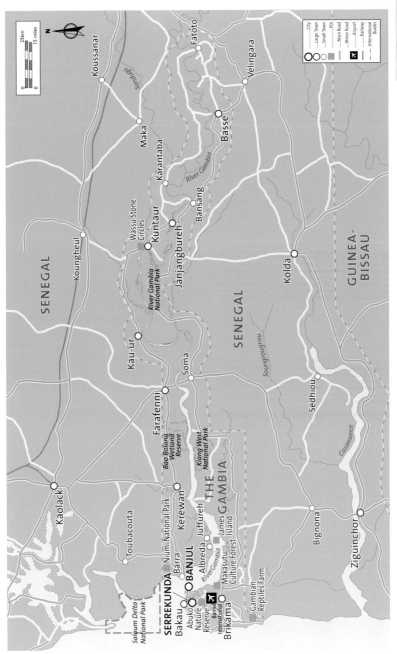

Navigable for almost 600km (373 miles), the river was a useful conduit for early adventurers who could forge their way in dugout canoes into the heart of the then unexplored continent. One fascinating element in the story of the river is its tidal reach, with the rhythmical rise and fall affecting over 520km (323 miles) of its length and saltwater intrusion reaching 200km (124 miles) inland. This tidal reach has always hindered human utilisation of the riverbanks. The salt inundation renders the soil useless for growing crops and tides prohibit settlement on the banks – villages, even fishing villages, are usually built some way from the water's edge.

Dense stands of mangroves extend on both sides of the river for over 160km (99 miles), with saltwater mangroves giving way to freshwater mangroves and deciduous forest the further east you travel. Hundreds of smaller inlets called *bolongs* extend from the mangroves and constitute an important ecosystem for wildlife.

Where the river once aided travel and navigation, today it hinders smooth travel around the country. The Gambia relies on a few slow and overworked ferries to get from north to south, a method that is becoming ever more outdated and inadequate.

The coast

The Gambia's 80km (50 miles) of coastline constitute some of Africa's westernmost land mass. Hundreds of square kilometres of mangroves protect the land from the sometimes violent Atlantic storms and act as a haven for birdlife both native and visiting. However, the mangroves give way to long swathes of sand on other stretches of the coast; beautiful beaches that have helped in the development of the tourist industry. The beaches are, however, one of The Gambia's most fragile environments, prone to being washed away by strong offshore currents and the aforesaid storms.

Land use

Only 27 per cent of The Gambia's land is suitable for farming, though this could be improved if irrigation systems were more widespread. Around 75 per cent of

PRACTICAL PLANTS

Gambians still live in close harmony with their land and have learnt to utilise many trees and plants in the household.

The baobab is very useful. Gambians eat the fruit and pounded leaves are mixed with couscous to make it more digestible. The flesh of the fruit is soaked in water and the liquid is used to relieve bowel pain.

The leaves of the neem tree are boiled and the juice is used to treat the symptoms of malaria. Pounded leaves are added to soap and used to kill hair lice.

Rice husks are a natural irritant to termites. Stinking pea is pounded into powder and used as an insecticide and rodent poison. Sodom apple leaves drive rodents away. Cassia leaves added to linen stores protect textiles from cockroaches and termites. Strip the bark of the grey plum tree and soak it in water for a natural non-fizzy cola.

Tending crops in Busumbale

the population still makes a living from the land, so improvements in water use will directly affect the livelihoods of over a million people. Groundnuts or peanuts are the major crop, but others include rice, millet, sesame, cassava (tapioca) and palm kernels.

Regular flooding of upland plateau areas during the rainy season makes them ideal for growing crops, though the highest plateaus, only a few metres above this band, are too dry. Rainfall has fallen 30 per cent in the last 20 years, making increased desertification a major concern. Villages tend to be located in the band between the tidal flows of the river and the land irrigated by the summer rains, meaning women and children must walk long distances daily to tend and harvest the crops.

Almost 30 per cent of the land is classed as woodland and forest, though this percentage is dropping. The major deciduous hardwoods, including mahogany and ebony, are now prized worldwide, so the government has introduced legislation to protect the last remaining areas and farmers must replant young trees if they wish to harvest mature specimens.

Around the forests and farmland are vast tracts of savanna grasslands, covered in *Pennisetum purpureum*, or elephant grass, which can reach 4.5m (15ft) in height and which Gambians cut for thatch and fencing. The mighty baobab is the king of the savanna, punctuating the skyline; other leviathans include the silk cottonwood tree, or kapok tree, and the acacia.

History

c. **800** BC	The earliest settlers, thought to be ancestors of the present-day Jola, arrive in the region.
c. AD **500**	The region falls under the influence of the Kingdom of Ghana.
c. **1000**	Senegambia is converted to Islam.
c. **1400**	The Mandinka rule the Senegambia region from their kingdom in Mali.
1447	Portuguese explorer Nuno Tristão ventures into the River Gambia region.
1457	A Portuguese delegation establishes a trading post on St Andrew's Island (now James Island).
1588	The Portuguese sell trade rights on the River Gambia to the British.
1618	King James of England and Scotland grants a charter to a British company to set up trading posts.
1651	The Duchy of Courland (*see pp12–13*) establishes a trading post on the river.
1661	The Duchy of Courland loses control of the trading post due to war in northern Europe.
1783	The Treaty of Versailles gives Great Britain possession of The Gambia, with the French retaining Albreda on the north bank.
1807	Parliament in London bans slavery throughout the British Empire.
1816	Bathurst is established at the mouth of the River Gambia.
1816–88	The Gambia is controlled by the British Governor General based in Sierra Leone.
1857	Albreda is ceded to the British.
1888	Gambian territory becomes a separate colonial entity ruled from Bathurst.
1889	France accepts the established borders of The Gambia and the territory is declared a British Crown Colony.

1939–45 The Gambia becomes an important staging post for naval convoys heading for the Cape of Good Hope and air convoys run by the US Army Air Corps. As a French colony, surrounding Senegal was considered enemy territory, so The Gambia was on a constant state of high alert.

1962 General elections held.

1963 The Gambia becomes self-governing.

1965 The Gambia becomes independent on 18 February. It joins the Commonwealth of Nations as a constitutional monarchy.

1970 The Gambia becomes a republic within the Commonwealth and Sir Dawda Kairaba Jawara becomes head of state.

1973 Bathurst becomes Banjul.

1982 The Senegambia Confederation between Senegal and The Gambia is announced. Under the agreement the two countries aim to unify their economies and defence structures.

1989 The Gambia withdraws from the Senegambia Confederation.

1994 On 22 July Jawara is toppled in a military coup organised by the Armed Forces Provisional Ruling Council. Lieutenant Yahya A J J Jammeh becomes head of state.

1996 Elections vote Jammeh as president of the newly constituted Republic of The Gambia.

2001 Jammeh is re-elected.

2004 Deyda Hydara, a leading journalist opposed to President Jammeh, is assassinated.

2006 In March a military coup plot is uncovered and the army chief flees the country. Jammeh is re-elected for a third term in September.

2010 Death penalty introduced for possession of cocaine or heroin.

2011 Presidential elections due.

The Latvian connection – a short history of the Duchy of Courland

The small Baltic state of Latvia was for many generations alive with territorial machinations, but the rise of the Duchy of Courland is its most fascinating story. It's the tale of a family with a nose for business, set against a backdrop of friction between second-millennium political powerbrokers.

The Duchy was born out of the death throes of the Livonia Confederation and occupied a tract of land west of the Daugava River extending to the Baltic coast, now part of modern Latvia. Courland was one of a handful of minor duchies over which Sweden and Poland vied for control.

Gottard Kettler (1561–87), last Master of the Order of Livonia, became the first Duke of Courland in 1516, and he was followed by his sons. Under the early Kettlers, mining and shipbuilding became big business. However, it was the era of Jacob Kettler (1642–82) that brought the Duchy to international attention. At its peak it was less a geographical entity than one of the world's first 'corporations', and Jacob was the Richard Branson or Donald Trump of his day.

He travelled extensively in Europe, extending trading ties. One of the Duchy's major industries was gunpowder, a vital resource for colonial powers, and Courland sold to the major players: Britain, France and Portugal. Jacob built his own trading fleet, and as a mercantile sea-power he took a step into the 'big league' in 1651, founding a colony on St Andrew's Island in the River Gambia, where he built a fort (see pp68–71). In 1652 Jacob founded a second overseas colony on Tobago in the

Cannons by the jetty on James Island (formerly St Andrew's Island)

Fort James (formerly Jacob) ruins

West Indies, from where he began to trade sugar, tobacco and coffee.

Unfortunately, all this activity and increased wealth caught the attention of both the Poles and the Swedes. In 1655, the Swedes invaded Courland and the Poles came to defend the territory, starting the Swedish–Polish War (1655–60). Jacob was taken prisoner, and his fleet and most of the Duchy's industrial base was destroyed.

The Duchy never really recovered from this conflict, with Jacob's son Friedrich Casimir skimming off the profits to fund a glamorous court. When he died in 1698 his successor Friedrich Wilhelm was only six years old and was controlled by a Polish regent. As a Polish ally, the Duchy was drawn into conflict again with Sweden, on the side of Russia, during the Great Northern War (1700–21). Friedrich Wilhelm made the astute move of aligning himself to Peter the Great by marrying into the Russian royal family. Unfortunately, on the journey back from his wedding in St Petersburg in 1711 he fell ill and died, and the Kettlers lost control of their Duchy.

Friedrich Wilhelm left a vacuum behind, with both Poland and Russia backing rival claimants. Eventually, however, heavily backed by Friedrich's widow (by now Anna I of Russia), one Ernst von Biron, an *évolué* native of Courland reputed to be the lover of the Empress, was appointed Duke in 1737. Biron handed over control of the territory to his son Peter in 1769, but by this time Russia and Poland were entering a period of protracted friction and Peter was happy to cede his territory to Russia in 1795, signalling the end of the Duchy of Courland.

Politics

Politics in The Gambia has been dominated by one larger-than-life character since the mid-1990s. After winning a third term in office in late 2006, President Yahya Abdul-Aziz Jemus Junkung Jammeh has plans to turn his country into an oil-rich, self-sufficient state, despite the fact that not a drop of the black stuff has ever been extracted from Gambian territory.

Jammeh was born on 25 May 1965 and joined the former National Gendarmerie in 1984 after passing several 'O' levels at Gambia High School. He rose through the ranks, taking on high-profile roles in personal surveillance and the security of politicians and visiting dignitaries, reaching the rank of Lieutenant before the military coup that ousted the democratically elected government of Dawda Jawara in 1994. As Chairman of the Armed Forces Provisional Ruling Council who organised the coup, he took control of the country in the immediate aftermath, then retired from the military to take up life as a politician.

Jammeh has pretty much ruled single-handedly since then. After the coup, all political parties with strong ties to the previous Jawara regime were banned, so Jammeh's Alliance for Patriotic Reorientation and Construction won the first election under the new constitution. The parties were reinstated in 2001, but by this time Jammeh had strong control over the media and a high profile across the country.

Since then, Jammeh's grip on power has tightened and a cult of personality has begun to overshadow party politics. Several sets of new media laws since the turn of the millennium have restricted freedom of the press even further. In 2004 these new laws allowed the government to imprison journalists found guilty of libel and sedition. Vocal opponent of the legislation and newspaper proprietor Deyda Hydara was shot dead only days after the law came into force.

In 2005 three leading opposition politicians were arrested as part of an undercover operation looking into threats against the regime, and in March 2006, 27 Gambians including top army officers and government officials were arrested for planning to topple the president. A number escaped into neighbouring Senegal, whose government Jammeh accuses of trying to undermine his regime.

There has been tension between the governments of The Gambia and Senegal on and off since the Senegambia Confederation crumbled in 1989. Senegal is desperate to see a bridge built across the River Gambia, to improve communications between Dakar and its own Casamance province south of Gambian territory, where freedom fighters undermine Senegal's own borders.

Since his most recent election success in September 2006, President Jammeh has continued to plough an individualist furrow through international relations. In December 2006 he made a three-day visit to Iran to meet with President Ahmadinejad and defended Iran's right to develop nuclear weapons. In January 2007, the president announced that he had been given a mandate from the spirit world to cure illnesses, including asthma and HIV, through herbal potions and the laying on of hands. Long queues of expectant patients now form outside State House on the morning of Jammeh's 'surgeries', but scientists and doctors across Africa are appalled by this turn of events.

Jammeh's already poor human rights record took a further dive in May 2008, when he publicly announced that he would 'cut off the head' of any homosexual found in The Gambia. Then, in March 2009, hundreds of Gambians were kidnapped during a government campaign against so-called witchcraft, a campaign in which Jammeh denies having any part. During the kidnappings, victims were jailed and forced to drink concoctions purported to exorcise evil spirits.

In October 2010, the government introduced the death penalty for those found guilty of possessing cocaine or heroin, in an effort to discourage the international drug trafficking that is on the rise in West Africa and a matter of serious concern. Gambians will again go to the polls for a new president (Jammeh has stated that he will not be standing) in September 2011, giving the citizens of this beautiful and fascinating, yet politically compromised, country the opportunity to put a more democratic, tolerant and progressive government into power.

The Gambian flag

Bumsters – friends or foes?

With a lively patter and a 'never say die' attitude, 'bumsters' are a ubiquitous part of the holiday scene on The Gambia's tourist coast. They operate on the fringes of the tourist industry, hoping to take a slice of the cash it generates.

For many first-timers to The Gambia, the attentions of bumsters are the one negative in an otherwise enjoyable holiday. But many people who return to the country year after year feel that the bumsters are getting a raw deal. They have made friends with many of them, seeing them simply as genial guys trying to make a living.

A smiling beach bumster

Some bumsters hang around the tourist resorts hoping to pick up work as a guide, or touting for a restaurant or a boat trip. Other young fit men hang around the beaches – women holidaying without men will almost certainly get plenty of attention – and for those women of 'a certain age', The Gambia has a reputation for being a place where you can find very attentive holiday escorts.

Control and licensing

In the last few years the government has recognised that bumsters are one of the major causes of negative feedback about their country and a great deal has been done to clean up the business. A licensing system has been introduced to help visitors identify the professionals, and official 'Tourist Guides' can be found in or close to all the major hotels; you can hire them by the hour, the day or longer.

On the beaches, licensed fruit sellers and souvenir stalls have been installed in cute little tropical-style kiosks, and their proprietors don't roam along the beach touting for business. Even the juice pressers have an association. The latest buzz words are professionalism and sustainability.

A bumster on the beach at Sanyang

How to deal with bumsters

These steps have made a big difference since 2000, but still, even with the licensing of some vendors, you are bound to be approached on the beach or on the tourist strips as you sunbathe or head out to find something to eat. Often the guys will sidle up with a friendly hello and engage you on how your day is going – looking for a conversation-starter before pushing their services. There's no need to feel afraid or intimidated – they are not aggressive – but you'll need to be firm if you want to be left alone. This may happen several times during the course of the day so it's easy to become short-tempered if you feel you can't get a moment to yourself, but here are a few tips to help you cope.

Be polite but firm

- Don't say 'maybe' if you mean 'no'; bumsters remember.
- Keep smiling and wish them a good day.
- Tell them you hope they find some good business but you are not interested.
- Start as you mean to go on and stay true to your word. Bumsters will respect a 'no' expressed in a confident manner.

A final word

If you feel that a bumster has stepped over the line and is harassing rather than persuading, you can file a report with the tourist police (*see p147*). This special force has been set up specifically to help visitors with nuisance or crime.

Culture

Cultural norms in The Gambia are very different to those in Europe or North America. Exploring these differences is one of the most fascinating elements of a visit to the country. The people of 'The Smiling Coast' are happy to tell you about their lives and their communities in which, outside the main towns, life has changed little for many generations.

The Gambian village

Families live in compounds made up of several huts surrounded by a fence for privacy and security. Very few compounds have fresh water, so in the country villages are serviced by a community well, while towns use standpipes. Most compounds don't have electricity either, so families socialise around small *attaya* stoves in summer and around fires that are used to provide warmth on cool winter evenings. Tasks are divided according to gender. The men are responsible for the rebuilding and re-thatching of the compound huts, and for planting at the start of the rainy season. They also spend lots of time seated on the *bantaba*, a large seating area at the heart of the village, where the business of the day is discussed and much time is spent in jocular wordplay or in games of backgammon (*see p20*). Women are responsible for tending and harvesting crops, collecting water, cooking, childcare and all domestic chores.

BANTABA

Bantaba is the origin of the English word banter, meaning 'a friendly exchange of teasing remarks'. The *Oxford English Dictionary* states that the word is '17th century: origin unknown', but the date certainly tallies with the arrival of the British in the region.

Religion

Over 90 per cent of the Gambian population is Muslim, with a minority of Christians – denominations range from Catholic to Anglican, Wesleyan to Seventh-day Adventist. However, although monotheism is an important element in life, many Gambians also infuse their beliefs with a pagan animism (belief that supernatural powers influence life) symbolised by the use of spells and *jujus* (charms imbued with powers). The fortune-teller/herbalist/witch doctor is a much-revered individual, especially in Jola society (*see p22*), and is consulted about all manner of things from the timing of travel to the

A typical rural village

wisdom of business deals. Many Gambians wear a talisman to protect against evil spirits. The veneration of the crocodile, including visiting their pools, is a practice that predates the deities.

Body culture

Breasts are not considered sexual parts of the body in Western Africa and you may see women breast-feeding without embarrassment when you visit villages. The most erotic parts of a woman's body are considered to be the thighs, which is why women wear long dresses or skirts that flow over these areas rather than drawing attention to them by wearing skimpy skirts.

Marriage

Polygamy is legal in The Gambia and it's not unusual for a man to have two or three wives living in the family compound. The husband has his own hut or bedroom and is visited by each wife in turn for two nights before he takes a night's rest. Not surprisingly, Gambian males set great store in the restorative effects of plants like African laburnum, which are touted as a natural form of Viagra.

Marriages are usually arranged by the parents of the couple, though not against the will of the couple themselves. Traditionally, negotiations take place between the male heads of household after an initial gift of kola

TEA CEREMONY

Brewing Gambian tea or *attaya* is a time-honoured ritual that punctuates all social and ceremonial occasions, and forms an important activity when friends get together after dark. To start the process, you'll need a small enamel teapot and a small square charcoal burner, easily bought at all Gambian markets.

Attaya is made using green gunpowder tea from China. Put one whole packet in the teapot with a small amount of water and sugar and let it boil on the burner. Pour the tea into a small glass tumbler, then pour it backwards and forwards into another tumbler until a foam develops. This foam should be equal to the volume of tea. Then sip the tea loudly through the foam. Each packet of tea is used to make three brews. The first and strongest is traditionally for the men. The second brew is weaker and has more sugar added, so it is said to be the woman's drink. The third is weakest and sweetest, for children and the elderly.

nuts is received by the woman's parents, and the marriage contract also involves more presents of nuts, cash and/or other goods. The woman's family must provide her with all the things she'll need to set up home. Sometimes it is many months between the ceremony and the wife moving to the man's compound, as families raise sufficient funds for these dowries.

Circumcision

Circumcision in males is universal in The Gambia and over 80 per cent of females are also circumcised, usually between the ages of eight and twelve. Aside from the question of whether this is a necessary and ethical practice, circumcision has always marked the passage from childhood to adulthood in Gambian society and is accompanied by long and grave initiation regimes.

As far as boys are concerned, to commence the process they traditionally depart the village to attend 'bush school', where an elder teaches them the rules and behaviours expected of them as adults, including sex education. At bush school the boys are protected by *kangkurang* (if they are Mandinka) or *kumpo* (for the Jola) spirit guides who keep evil spirits at bay. They are then circumcised by the village blacksmith, and after a period of recuperation return to their compounds where their families throw a big party to celebrate their new status and welcome them back into the world. Circumcised boys sleep in a separate hut away from the women until they take a wife of their own. Today, bush school is much less popular, especially in the Kombos (western coastal areas), and many elders point to this change as one of the reasons for the kinds of ills that seem to have befallen society, including crime, spousal abuse and rude behaviour.

TOUBAB

Toubab is the Wolof word meaning 'white man'. It is now used by people of all Gambian ethnic groups to describe light-skinned visitors of either sex, and you'll most often here it shouted by children as they wave excitedly at you from their village compounds.

Gambian women tend to wear long, flowing dresses

The tribes of The Gambia

Society in The Gambia is made up of a number of discrete ethnic groups who are found not only here but across a whole swathe of Western Africa. Many Gambians have family ties in neighbouring French-speaking Senegal, Mali and beyond.

Mandinka

By far the most widespread of The Gambia's peoples, the Mandinka make up more than 40 per cent of the total population.

Mandinka society is hierarchical, ruled by age and social standing – there has also traditionally been a ruling noble clan. Their history is passed down through the *griots,* a clan of *kora*-playing storytellers.

Mandinka men wear a brimless cap and a voluminous kaftan over loose

Mandinka ritual performer

trousers, while women wear tight-fitting 'bodiced' dresses with plunging backs, ruffled sleeves and slight bustles – inspired by the fashions of the European colonial women during the 18th and 19th centuries.

Jola

The Jola are thought to have been the earliest arrivals to the region. The most animist of the tribes – even though they are mostly Muslim – there is still a deep belief in, and production of, *jujus (see pp128–9)* spells and magical potions. The Jola traditionally lived in large villages of several thousand individuals, without a tribal chief or ruling clan.

One clan of the Jola is the Manjago, who traditionally undertake 'palm tapping'. The Manjago are Christian and/or animist and are also the only clan to keep pigs.

Jola men wear baggy trousers and shirts with waistcoats. The women's headdress has a corner which falls over the face.

Fula

Widespread across Western Africa, the Fula are the second-largest group in the country. Traditionally cattle herders, they led a semi-nomadic

A traditional healer (witch doctor) from Tunjina

Wolof men wear long kaftans and the women look striking in their colourful and voluminous full-length dresses worn over a full-length skirt, and high head-ties.

Wolof men are renowned for being skilled drummers.

Serahule

Rulers of the Kingdom of Ghana and the pre-eminent tradesmen of West Africa, the Serahule arrived in The Gambia in the 19th century as refugees, escaping war in their own country. Traders in gold and silver, the women wear large gold earrings decorated with red cord.

existence and accumulated few possessions. One example of this is their main instrument, the *riti* – a type of flute that was easily transportable.

Fula women sport large quantities of gold jewellery and have tattoos around the mouth or on the face. Men wear tunics of rough cotton and conical straw hats.

Serer

One of the oldest tribes in Senegambia, the Serer are traditionally fishermen. Their heartland is in the Nuimi district around Barra on the north shore. According to oral history, they were enslaved by the Fula.

Wolof

A minority within the country's population, the Wolof are thought to have descended from African royalty and reached The Gambia from Mauritania. They dominated trade and are now heavily involved in tourism. Traditional Wolof society was hierarchical with many castes. Today, social standing is measured more by wealth or education.

Aku

Descendants of freed slaves that returned to Africa in the 19th century, the Aku are often mixed race, the result of liaisons between slave women and colonial slave masters, and have names such as Williams, Barry or Jones. They speak Creole, rather than an African tribal language, and their English is often very good.

Festivals and events

Celebrations in The Gambia range from the all-singing, all-dancing national events such as Independence Day, to more intimate family occasions that commemorate important life stages.

National events

Independence Day (18 February)

The main event is held in Banjul with military parades and marches centred on July 22 Square; however, all the main towns have some sort of official parade or event.

Kanilai Cultural Festival (every odd year, end May)

Inaugurated to coincide with the president's birthday on the 25th, this cultural festival celebrates all things Gambian with traditional songs and dances, and is an opportunity to see authentic Gambian wrestling.

The International Roots Festival (every even year, one week during June)

The biggest event of the calendar, when The Gambia throws open its doors to its African American brethren and the African Diaspora travel over for a spiritual and very emotional homecoming. Hundreds arrive in Juffureh to re-enact the final moments of Kunta Kinte (*see p76*) and to meet with the family. They are welcomed by hundreds of villagers from *griots* (*see p22*) and elders to schoolchildren. But beyond the historical north-shore locations, the whole of The Gambia erupts into life with cultural concerts and tribal dancing, culinary festivals and special markets – the whole country seems to get involved.

Revolution Day (22 July)

To commemorate the coup that ousted the previous regime in 1994, President Jammeh gives a rousing speech and there are nationwide celebrations.

Religious festivals

Milad al-Nabi

The Prophet Muhammad's birthday is spent in reflection with readings from the Koran and messages from the Imam.

Koriteh

This feast marks the end of Ramadan, the yearly period of fasting. Muslims start the day with prayers and then there is a huge celebratory meal when family and friends dress up and get together. Koriteh is a time when family members working away will try to get home, which puts tremendous strain on bush taxi systems throughout the country.

Tobaski (Tabaski)

The Feast of the Sacrifice coincides with The Hajj pilgrimage to Mecca and takes place two months and ten days after the end of Ramadan. The head of the family sacrifices a goat, as Ismail did, and the family sit down to give thanks. This is another festival where family members working away from home return, even if only for the day.

Social and family festivals
Circumcision rite of passage

After girls and boys have undergone circumcision (*see p20*) and spent time in bush school, they return home to their families as adults. In their absence, the family will have prepared new clothes and shoes. There's also a huge family feast with *masquerede* dancing at which costumed, masked or stilted guides such as the *kankurang* or *kumpo* appear to keep away evil spirits.

Naming Day Ceremony

The Naming Day marks the official welcome of a new baby into society, and it's an important social occasion for the individual and for the family. One week after the birth, the elders of the village gather at the family compound. A tribal elder cuts a lock of the baby's hair and an animal is sacrificed as the name is said. In Mandinka families a *griot* or *jeli* sings traditional songs during the ceremony. The family and friends then sit down to a meal and the celebrations go on into the night with traditional drumming, singing and dancing.

Many events are celebrated with music and dancing

Highlights

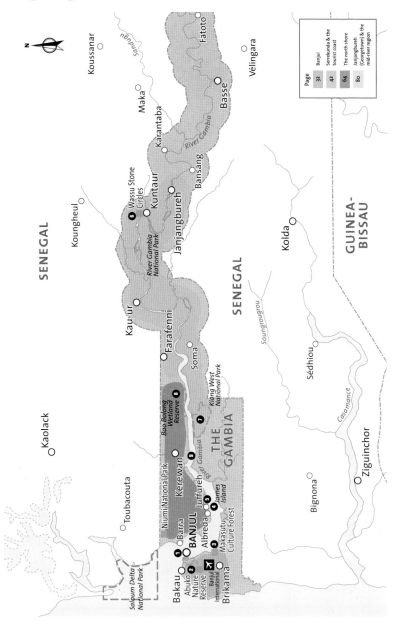

1 **Albert Market, Banjul** Shopping in Albert Market in Banjul, the capital's lively open-air bazaar, offers a rich slice of West African daily life (*see pp33–4*).

2 **Abuko Nature Reserve** Exploring Abuko Nature Reserve, the most accessible of The Gambia's many protected natural areas (*see pp43–5*).

3 **Makasutu Culture Forest** Touching the trees in the Makasutu Culture Forest; this sacred place is now an award-winning eco-attraction (*see pp52–4*).

4 **Stepping onto James Island** Many thousands of Africans left this small island for a life of slavery in the 'New World' (*see pp68–71*).

5 **Kinte clan at Juffureh** Shaking the hand of the head of the Kinte clan at Juffureh, descendants of Kunta Kinte, the first of *Roots* author Alex Haley's relatives to land on American soil to be sold into slavery (*see pp74–5*).

6 **Wassu Stone Circles** Gazing at the Wassu Stones, the most ancient man-made structures in the country and the only evidence of a long-lost society (*see p91*).

7 **Kiang West National Park** Tramping through the forest of Kiang West National Park, the most diverse ecosystem in The Gambia, protecting more flora and fauna than any other in the country (*see pp86–7*).

8 **Bao Bolong Wetland Reserve** Discovering the inlets of Bao Bolong Wetland Reserve, a world-renowned wetland area and a haven for wading birds (*see pp65–7*).

9 **River Gambia cruises** Cruising on the River Gambia, to enjoy the tempo of life on the water that is the lifeblood of the country (*see p28*).

10 **Village life** Visiting a Gambian village, to learn about life in the rural heartland (*see pp99–101*).

A musician playing *kora* music at Makasutu Culture Forest

Suggested itineraries

Despite the fact that The Gambia is a small country, travelling times should never be underestimated and will play a large part in deciding where you visit during your trip, however much time you have. With many of the country's best attractions being both natural and unpredictable (animals and birds don't appear on cue), factoring in time and flexibility is an absolute must. This is one destination where you can't expect travel plans to go 100 per cent smoothly, especially if you want to leave the coast and explore inland.

A long weekend or midweek break

If you intend to spend only a short time in the country – a long weekend of four or so days – you'll be better off staying in the western coastal areas: the district known as Kombo or the Kombos. You are sure to want to enjoy the beach for at least part of your trip and you should plan for a day or a couple of afternoons of doing absolutely nothing but relaxing by the sea.

Spend a morning exploring the capital; shopping in Albert Market introduces you to West African urban life. Take in the atmosphere of the bustling alleyways and snack on peanuts or cashew nuts (grown in the countryside here) as you browse.

It's also important to spend some time on the river, so book a cruise in a traditional wooden pirogue. Early birds can catch the morning chorus (but it does mean getting to the boat by 6.45am), otherwise you can take a mid-afternoon trip. Either way you'll spend three or four hours among the mangroves with only birdsong and the tapping of oyster fisherwomen's machetes breaking the silence.

Abuko Nature Reserve is the closest protected tract of land to the coastal strip, so it's easy to reach by taxi and you can then spend as much time as you like exploring and watching the birds, monkeys, crocodiles and deer. Makasutu Culture Forest offers similar scenery but has several differences to Abuko, not least of which is the delicious buffet lunch that's served in the restaurant (pre-book or arrive as part of a group) and the wooden deck where you can have a cooling drink and watch the activity on Mandina Bolong. Makasutu offers a chance to tour the *bolongs* (creeks) in dugout canoes, while the forest has a large troop of baboons that treat the man-made structures with disdain – great fun if you are lucky enough to be there when they come through. This sacred place is now an award-winning eco-attraction.

You should also take time to explore the traditional lifestyles of Gambians, and the easiest way to do this is to visit a village compound. It's a humbling experience to discover how simply the vast majority of the population lives, and to learn about daily life in Africa.

Don't forget to get out of the hotel in the evening to enjoy the bars and restaurants of the Senegambia Strip or the western end of Kairaba Avenue. The folkloric performance on Saturday evenings at Makasutu is also a must.

The major ground tour operators along the coast organise day tours incorporating several activities listed above on the same itinerary, with transport and lunch included. If you don't want the trouble of organising your time and transport yourself, this is a great way to discover the attractions of the Kombos.

A week

A few more days means you can factor in time to leave the Kombos and travel

Explore the *bolongs* of Makasutu in a pirogue

A hyena at Abuko Nature Reserve

upcountry (east towards central Africa). The most obvious extra activity is to follow the *Roots* trail and immerse yourself in the story of slavery in The Gambia. You can meet the African descendants of author Alex Haley at their family compound at Juffureh and take a trip to James Island, the British headquarters from where hundreds of thousands of Africans were taken against their will to the Caribbean and the Americas.

Another excursion allows you to visit Kanilai, birthplace of President Jammeh, to enjoy the Game Park and have lunch at Sindola Lodge.

Two weeks

Spending two weeks in The Gambia gives you enough time to visit much of the mid-river region in addition to enjoying the attractions on the coast. A four-to-six-night itinerary allows you to spend time at all of The Gambia's upcountry national parks and to visit the standing stone circles at Wassu.

On day one, once across the river, follow the north shore road to spend some time at Bao Bolong National Park before pushing on to reach your lodge at Janjangbureh (Georgetown) before nightfall. The next day, explore the town and retrace your steps to the north shore for the 15-minute journey to Wassu to see the ancient stones. Give day three over to a boat trip along the river to take in the River Gambia National Park and catch sight of chimps of the Rehabilitation Trust (*see pp88–9*) and hippos wallowing in the shallows, then return to Janjangbureh for the night. On day four prepare for the 'route from hell' as you tackle the southern arterial road heading back for the coast. Set off early to reach Tendaba by lunchtime, then take a boat trip or trek into Kiang West National Park, home to leopards and caracals, then stay overnight at Tendaba Camp. If you powered on past Bao Bolong on day one, you can get to the park by boat

from Tendaba, so perhaps allow for an extra day here. Finally, on day five (or six), return to the coast for a well-earned rest.

Longer?

The ultimate mode of transport for really getting under the skin of The Gambia is a wooden pirogue. This vessel allows you to travel with the rhythm of the river, hopping on and off to explore the countryside wherever you like. As nothing is very far from the water, you can take a bicycle and visit rural villages, allowing the local pace of life to pull you in. If you do want to make this a once-in-a-lifetime trip and include all of The Gambia's best attractions, you'll need to allow 10–14 days.

Local women in Janjangbureh

Banjul

When the British wanted to defend the mouth of the River Gambia against the French and Portuguese just after the abolition of slavery within the empire, they built a fortress on either bank. St Mary's Island, the most northerly point of dry land on the south bank, had its advantages, being protected by an impenetrable maze of mangrove bolongs on its western flank – so Bathurst was born in 1816. Over time the settlement blossomed into the capital, which was renamed Banjul in 1973.

Not without its charms, Banjul has suffered a great reversal of fortune in the modern age, hemmed in as it is by a veritable swathe of mangrove, known as the Tanbi Wetlands, that proved such an asset 150 years before. It couldn't contain the burgeoning population and most made the decision to move to less crowded accommodation around Serrekunda to the west. Today its permanent population is less than 40,000.

See pp38–9 for Walk route.

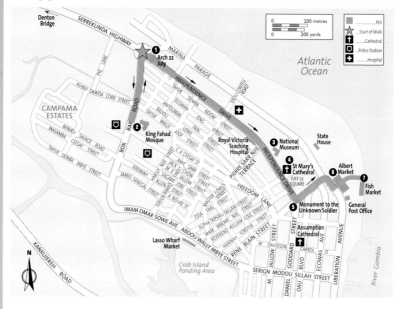

During daylight hours Banjul seethes with activity. Hundreds of civil servants head to desk jobs in government departments, nurses to shifts at the country's teaching hospital, the Royal Victoria, and secondary-school pupils to lessons at Gambia Senior Secondary School. Almost every fisherman, shopkeeper, market trader and shopper lives outside the city and travels in and out daily along the one arterial road cutting through the mangrove, packed into old, noisy bush taxis and buses. Add to this the foot and heavy goods traffic from ferries linking Banjul to Barra on the north coast (one of only three places where commercial traffic can cross the river, and a major conduit for traffic from northern Senegal and southern Senegal) and you have organised chaos. You think that your commute is difficult? Just wait until you witness this!

Sandy swathes bound the city on its northern and western flanks from where a colourful fishing fleet heads out to sea. From here it's possible to take in the immense size of the river just before it disgorges into the sea. Across the gaping mouth one can just make out the town of Barra on the north bank.

Albert Market

Aside from its role as a capital, Banjul has one raison d'être: trade. The streets are lined with shops, and impromptu stalls pop up on every street corner selling everything from towels to fake watches. Vendors even stroll the streets

Albert Market

selling goods out of suitcases; it's the deal that counts. The best place to really soak in this mercantile atmosphere is at Albert Market, a huge labyrinth of permanent stalls supplemented by thousands of smallholders selling freshly picked fruit and vegetables beautifully displayed on a piece of clean cloth set out on the ground. Vendors and customers cram together and stevedores steer through the melée, barrows piled high with produce. Fruit and vegetables, fish and meat, each has its own section; then there are fabrics, clothes, toiletries and numerous curious objects and produce that you'll just need to guess at, like the thin sticks of wood that Gambians use to clean their teeth, or grotesque-looking roots to be boiled in water and said to be as powerful as Viagra. Albert Market has a large craft and souvenir section and the

Arch 22 July marks the military coup of 1994

stallholders are a jovial crowd. Most of the merchandise is mass-produced – colourful bangles and necklaces or wooden carvings of animals – though there are a couple of stalls selling good-quality drums and other African instruments. If you find something you like, you'll need to bargain hard to get a good price.

Liberation Avenue. Open: daily 8am–7pm.

Arch 22 July

Banjul's most visible edifice was commissioned by President Jammeh to commemorate the military coup that brought him to power and 'liberated' The Gambia on 22 July 1994. The arch was designed to stand as a monument to the founding of a new, forward-looking regime; however, with an

estimated price tag of just over one million US dollars, some might argue that the money would have been better spent elsewhere.

Designed by Pierre Goudiaby, a Senegalese architect and favourite of Jammeh, the arch spans the northern end of Independence Drive and marks the entrance to the city from the main highway. Eight mammoth Doric columns, large enough to house lifts and spiral staircases, support the main structure. Sadly, the lifts are no longer working because settlement into the soft substrate has caused the shafts to change shape.

Climb the stairs to the intermediate level where the terrace offers excellent views across the Banjul skyline. From here the single-storey, corrugated-roofed family homes form a dense patchwork interspersed with low-rise office buildings. You get a real feel for how small the city is, something that's difficult to grasp when you are trying to negotiate the crowded streets.

Unfortunately, because traffic isn't allowed to pass beneath it (except for the cars of high government officials), the arch causes long queues at adjacent road intersections. On the north side are the gardens decorated with statues of traditional musicians by Goudiaby's brother; these were originally gilded but have now completely lost their glossy veneer.

Independence Drive. Open: daily 8am–4pm. Admission charge.

Denton Bridge

The only crossing point linking Banjul with the rest of southern Gambia, Denton Bridge is busy with traffic throughout the day. There's little of interest here, but the jetties on the inland side of the bridge are the home bases for most of the boats that tour the *bolongs* – so most people who book a boat trip will find themselves here at one time or another – be it for 'Birds and Breakfast' at 5.30am or a 'Sunset Cruise' at 5.30pm. This makes Denton Bridge the gateway to a whole different Gambia; one of tidal mangroves, sandbanks, herons and ospreys, and the relative silence of the natural world.

On the western approach 5km (3 miles) from Banjul.

Boats near Denton Bridge

King Fahad Mosque

The Gambia's largest mosque was built with funds gifted by the King of Saudi Arabia, after whom it is named, and it opened in 1988. It's a total contrast to the many intimate neighbourhood and village mosques where a hundred or so people might gather at Friday lunchtime for the main weekly prayer meeting. At King Fahad Mosque there's a large internal courtyard and an immense sandy outer courtyard with a capacity of thousands, and one can imagine the impression these masses of people praying together would have on a first-time visitor.

Still, most of the time the mosque is a very quiet place. The architectural form is elegant, with beige stucco emphasising the clean lines. However, its main impact is in its size; the twin minarets punctuate the skyline, visible even as you arrive by air, and the overall structure is the largest in the city.
Box Bar Road. Open: dawn–dusk except during prayer times. Free admission.

National Museum

Housed in the old Bathurst Club building, where colonial stalwarts would meet for a G&T and listen to cricket on the radio, this is the country's principal national collection. A range of artefacts chronicling the history of Senegambia, both geologically and anthropologically, with a little imagination the displays could offer much, but in reality they interest few. There are treasures to be found, however, especially for anyone with an interest in the development of Africa as a continent, particularly the ground-floor exhibits from The Gambia pre- and post-Independence. There's an interesting display charting the development of early societies in the region and background information about the arrival of Islam.

The collection ranges from the usual (old maps of the country and historical documents) to the bizarre, such as the dress worn by Miss Gambia when she won her beauty contest in 1984.
Independence Drive. Open: Mon–Thur 8am–4pm, Fri & Sat 8am–1pm. Admission charge.

St Mary's Cathedral

This unassuming painted-brick church, completed in the 1930s, is the centre for Anglican worship in The Gambia. Kept neat and tidy by the small Protestant community, it sees far fewer worshippers than it did during colonial rule.

The decorative highlight of the simple interior is an ornate tapestry depicting scenes from the Bible transposed into the African landscape.

To the right of the cathedral as you look towards the façade is July 22 Square, a parade ground renamed after the military coup. Today it's the venue for lavish Independence Day ceremonies and other celebrations, when President Jammeh takes place of honour along with other dignitaries in the grandstand on the western flank.

Close by on West Davidson Carrol Street is **Our Lady of the Assumption Cathedral**, completed in 1916 and the leading Catholic place of worship. *Independence Drive. Open: Mon–Sat 8am–7pm, Sun noon–7pm. Free admission.*

State House

The seat of the president sits on the northernmost point of St Mary's Island. In the grounds are the remains of Six-Gun Battery, the original cannon delivered to Bathurst when the city was founded. Unfortunately, even these were not powerful enough to fire missiles across the full width of the river, and enemy shipping merely hugged the north shore to avoid being hit. It was for this reason that **Fort Bullen** (*see p68*) was added on the north shore in the late 1820s.

State House. Not open to the public.

St Mary's Cathedral is a modest building

Walk: Downtown Banjul

Banjul is a compact capital brimming with activity. A stroll around introduces you to the energy of African life.

Allow 4 hours.

Distance: 5km (3 miles) including return to car.

See p32 for a map of the route.

Park your car on the verge of the street leading left from Arch 22 July (signposted Atlantic Hotel) – you'll be able to return to it later. Cross the street and you'll enter the small park at the top of Independence Drive.

1 Arch 22 July

Arch 22 July celebrates the military coup that brought the current president, Jammeh, to power in 1994. It dominates the cityscape rather like the bouffant hairstyle on the head of a slender woman. However, there are views across the whole city from the viewing platform on the intermediate level.
From the base of the arch, face down Independence Drive but don't walk down there just yet. Turn right down Box Bar Road for 300m (330yds) and you'll find King Fahad Mosque on the left.

2 King Fahad Mosque

King Fahad Mosque was built by money donated by the King of Saudi Arabia. It's the largest in The Gambia.

You can enter if it's not prayer time, but remember to remove your shoes and dress modestly.
Return to the arch and begin walking down Independence Drive. With government offices at the western end, it's free from all but official traffic, but just after the Royal Victoria Teaching Hospital, the route becomes busier. 700m (770yds) from Arch 22 July, you'll find the National Museum on the left.

3 National Museum

The Gambia's major anthropological and folkloric collection isn't the most impressive you'll ever see, but it does have some interesting social and religious artefacts to enjoy.
From the museum, continue walking east (away from the arch). After another 150m (160yds), the cream-painted St Mary's Cathedral sits at the roadside.

4 St Mary's Cathedral

The cathedral is a 1930s brick-built structure with a simple, serene interior.

The National Museum has some worthwhile exhibits

The pews are made out of fine mahogany, a wood now in short supply. *Continue your journey east once again. After the cathedral you'll pass July 22 Square, the venue for The Gambia's ebullient Independence Day parades. Just after the square, the road meets a main intersection.*

5 Monument to the Unknown Soldier

Traffic wheels around a small roundabout on which stands an almost forgotten but poignant monument to the Unknown Soldier.

Turn left at the intersection, keeping July 22 Square on your left. After 150m (160yds), cross the street and take a right down Liberation Avenue (also signposted Russell Street). The entrances to Albert Market are just on your left.

6 Albert Market

Albert Market is the best location to grasp the daily essence of life in modern Gambia. Take in the smells, sights and faces, and, of course, do a little shopping. Don't forget to haggle!

Leave the craft market section of Albert Market at the northeastern end and cross the grubby street to reach the beach. Turn right and you'll find the fishing fleet pulled up on the sand.

7 Fish Market

The fish market here is very busy in the early morning and the evening. Between times you'll find the women cleaning and preparing, and the men tending the nets.

After a refreshing drink at Omar's Beach Bar, the quickest way back to the car is to retrace your steps.

Boat tour from Denton Bridge

All vehicular traffic arriving or departing from Banjul has to cross Denton Bridge, which spans a large bolong *that cuts through the Tanbi wetlands. These wetlands offer hundreds of hectares of tidal mangrove replete with birdlife that seems a world away from the bustle of the capital. Most of the boat tours depart from Denton Bridge; the facility is simply a couple of wooden jetties with one unpretentious café.*

Allow 4 hours. Distance: 20km (12 miles).

Once you've made yourself comfortable the boat will depart, heading south along Oyster Creek.

1 Oyster Creek

The oyster harvesters work here, in the mangrove roots where the oysters

live, cutting them free with machetes. The women may spend many hours waist-deep in the water before finally returning to the shore to smoke their catch.

After 1km (¹⁄₂ mile), the boat takes a left turn down a meandering tributary called Turnbull Bolong.

2 Turnbull Bolong

Part of the north bank of this *bolong* is actually the southern boundary of Banjul Island; the impenetrable morass of mangrove is one of the reasons why the city could not expand beyond its constrictive boundaries. Turnbull Bolong offers close-quarter views of the mangrove banks. This is the place to spot Western Reef Herons and Whimbrels in the shallows, while Goliath Herons and Ospreys fly overhead.

After approximately 2km (1¹⁄₄ miles) Turnbull Bolong opens out into Chitabong Bolong.

3 Chitabong Bolong

The vista that greets your eyes here could be a seascape, but what you are actually looking at is the vast expanse of the River Gambia. It's over 20km (12 miles) directly across to the north shore from here, and often the long-distance view is shrouded in haze. To the north you'll see the southern tip of Banjul city, while the ferry dock at Barra is the most obvious landmark. *The boat turns right here, away from the capital and towards Chitabong, Daranka and Lamin islands.*

4 Iron-hulled Ships

The hulls of several old iron ships can be seen here. Left rotting in the shallows, they have become a favourite roost for pink-backed pelicans. *Beyond the islands, after 2.5km (1¹/₂ miles), the channel narrows and the boat makes its way into Lamin Bolong.*

5 Lamin Lodge

At the head of Lamin Bolong sits Lamin Lodge, for many years a popular stop en route for a swim or a drink. A true jungle shack made entirely of local wood, the lodge makes for an excellent photo opportunity. Look out for families of monkeys playing in the rafters. *From Lamin Lodge the boat heads home. After returning to the entrance of Lamin Bolong, it turns left into Daranka Bolong.*

6 Daranka Bolong

The leisurely journey back allows plenty more time for bird-spotting. Look out for chattering pied kingfishers, sacred ibises and perhaps a spoonbill or two. *Eventually, after 10km (6 miles), Daranka Bolong meets the intersection with Oyster Creek, and Denton Bridge will come into view ahead through the collection of masts. Your craft will draw quietly up to the jetty, bringing your trip to an end.*

Boat tour from Denton Bridge

The jungle shack at Lamin Lodge

Serrekunda and the tourist coast

The coast south of the River Gambia's mouth is the country's tourist heartland, where large resorts sit within metres of long, fine-sand beaches fringed with swaying palms. It's the stuff that holiday dreams are made of and the vast majority of The Gambia's visitors will book accommodation here, along a short stretch from Cape Point in the north down to Kololi in the south.

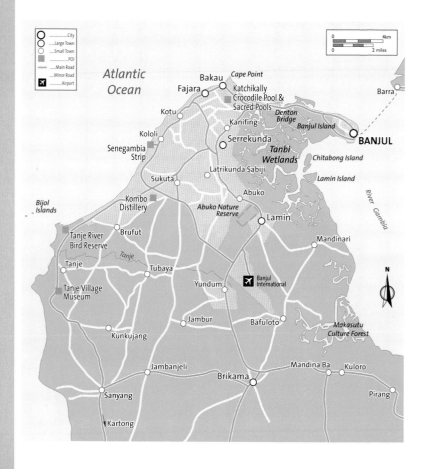

Vervet monkeys in Abuko Nature Reserve

Handfuls of inexpensive restaurants, beach bars and nightclubs make this a user-friendly tourist coast, but a certain something always reminds you that you're in Africa, be it the monkeys that flit across the roads or the booming of the drums – a sound that seems to rend the air, setting up a kind of Gambian heartbeat wherever you go.

But the Kombos, as the region is also known, offers much more than simple rest and relaxation. There are numerous attractions all along the verdant mangrove-swathed coastline or in the inland forests. You could fill a week with things to do, and ecotourism is beginning to make an impact with several small-scale sustainable projects set up by the indigenous communities.

Abuko Nature Reserve

The most accessible of The Gambia's protected areas, Abuko is an easy taxi ride from the resorts and offers a real opportunity to view some of the country's finest wildlife at close quarters. If you don't intend to visit any of the other national parks, then you should at least spend a couple of hours here, soaking up the real feel of wild Africa.

The reserve was created by conservation pioneer Eddie Brewer in the 1960s when he fenced a tract of savanna, tropical forest and gallery forest (woodland lining a stream or river) flanking the Lamin Bolong to protect the native trees and wildlife. Here you'll find one of very few year-round waterholes (called Bamboo Pool)

A makeshift bridge in the nature reserve

in the region, which supports many large tree species and attracts a whole range of animals, reptiles and birds – over 300 species have been spotted here. Abuko is one of the favoured rest stops for seasonal bird species that head into Europe in the summer months, and the park caters specifically to the needs of birdwatchers with several well-camouflaged hides. A single footpath snakes through the dense forest where you'll often find vervet monkeys scurrying along or foraging for food in the undergrowth. More secretive are the bushbuck deer, monitor lizards and crocodiles, which steer clear of human contact if at all possible.

The **Darwin Field Station**, close to Bamboo Pool, is an education centre for students of biodiversity who come here to study the animals. Non-academic visitors will find a wealth of information about the species that live here, with useful photographs and details about diet, habitat and behaviour. The balcony on the upper floor has great views across the waterhole, where, whatever the time of day, there is something fascinating to watch, be it the herons fishing in the shallows or snakes taking a welcome drink.

At the furthest reach of the footpath is a rather out-of-place **Animal Orphanage**, a wildlife rehabilitation facility set up in 1997 where baboons and other monkeys rescued from Gambian homes are supposedly being retrained to return to the wild. You'll also find a permanent population of well-fed hyenas lounging around, little troubled by the human visitors who stare at them through the fence.

For the best possible chance of seeing plenty of wildlife, arrive at Abuko early in the morning (before 10am) or late in the afternoon, because in the heat of the day the animals are much less active. For those more particularly interested in spotting wildlife, you can arrange visits outside normal park hours, when you may be rewarded by views of rare and shy native fauna.

On the main road south of Abuko village. Open: daily 8am–6pm. Admission charge.

Bakau

Like Serrekunda, Bakau has grown quickly in the last 20 years into a maze of narrow streets surrounding the nucleus of the old town. Most visitors make for the **Katchikally Crocodile Pool** (*see p49*) just to the south of town, but the real delight of a visit is its contrast with the tourist coastal strip just a couple of kilometres to the west. If you can rise above the constant *toubab*-ing (*see p20*) from endless herds of cheeky children, it's a fascinating introduction to everyday urban African life. Try the local market, which isn't as large as that at Serrekunda but offers a similar kind of atmosphere. The *bengdula* (*craft market*) is also much more user-friendly as all the stalls face the street rather than being arranged on an enclosed interior courtyard.

Craft market on Atlantic Road. Open: daily 9am–6pm.

The craft market in Bakau

Brikama

A centre of handicrafts, Brikama is famed for its woodcarvers. The output from small artisan-owned workshops in the town supplies most of the beach and street vendors on the Kololi coast, and many of the craft stalls in the markets. It's not surprising that when you visit the **craft market** here you can buy a full range of the wooden items found all across the country – from giraffes to tribal masks – but here you'll be able to chat to the people who carved them, many of whom have a talent passed down through generations of their families. Much of what you find 'front of shop' is the same as elsewhere along the coast, but if you want to avoid the kitsch, it's possible – the workshops lie just behind the area of the market stalls, and the smell of fresh sawdust is a delicate accompaniment to your tour.

Get into discussion with an artisan and ask them to carve you a bespoke piece; they'll relish and rise to the challenge. Just remember to agree a price first!

Wooden drums from Brikama

Most visitors to Fajara come for the golf

Brikama is also known throughout Senegambia for its musicians. Just as with woodcarving, many families have passed their musical talent through the generations and almost all current Gambian musical luminaries hail from the town (though they usually have to leave the country to build their careers). *Craft market. Main street.*
Open: daily 8am–7pm.

Fajara

This small coastal village, squeezed in between Bakau and Kotu, owes much to the period of British colonial rule, with architecture that speaks of bygone days. Though it's set among the tourist resorts, it still feels a world apart and many visitors race through in taxis heading for other places.

Golf is the main reason to visit Fajara. The **Fajara Country Club** maintains the Fajara Golf Club immaculately, even though the gardeners work to a different rule book to the greens keepers back home. There's a range of other sports to enjoy too.

The tiny **War Cemetery** in the village is a poignant memorial to those who lost their lives during World War II when Banjul was an important staging post for both shipping and air services. Over 300 people lie buried here and there is a memorial to over 30 Gambians who died on other battlefields during the conflict.
Fajara Country Club. Atlantic Road.
Tel: 449 5456. Greens open: daily.
War Cemetery. Kairaba Avenue.
Open access.

The Nile crocodile generally grows to around 4m (13ft) in The Gambia

Katchikally Crocodile Pool

The crocodile is a sacred animal to Gambians, revered for its great physical strength and its mystical powers. The waterholes frequented by Gambia's Nile crocodiles have become important in the country's animist rituals, and even today great care and attention are lavished on the beasts – particularly since the crocodiles' natural habitat is fast disappearing and they are becoming fewer in number.

Although it's not the only one in the region, the pool at Katchikally (also spelled Katchikali) is the most visited by tourists, with groups arriving regularly throughout the day. It might be easy to view this simply as another attraction, but your guide will be happy to go into greater detail about Gambian beliefs and rituals.

Katchikally has been made famous in modern times as the home of Charlie, the camera-hogging crocodile who just loves to have his photograph taken with visitors. Streams of people step up to shake paws with Charlie or to stroke his back. He seems unconcerned at the fuss. The guides assure you that Charlie has never attempted to attack a human, though one has to wonder what your travel insurance company would say if you had to make a claim!

Charlie is the photogenic crocodile, but he shares the pool with over 100 others, ranging in size from 50cm (20in) babies to 3m (10ft) giants. They float on the water surface among the bright-green pondweed or bask in the sunshine on the banks. A few herons also call the pond home, raising their chicks just a metre or so above a snout full of teeth, safe in the knowledge that few predators would dare to venture very close and risk being eaten by the giant reptiles.

Close to the entrance, the guardian family (*see box*) has created a small but very interesting folklore display featuring masks and musical instruments important to the local peoples, and information about the native plants and their uses.

Off Salt Matty Road, Bakau. Open: daily dawn–dusk. Admission charge.

THE SACRED POOLS

The crocodile is a powerful symbol in many West African cultures including those of all the peoples of The Gambia. A Mandinka legend states that a crocodile inhabits the moon, while others view the creature as a link between earthly life and the departed in the spirit world. Most prevalently, crocodiles are associated with fertility – the literal bringers of life, or the bestowers of good fortune and wealth.

Even today, infertile women come to bathe in the waters of the pool in a ritual designed to engender a pregnancy; businessmen too, who want success in a new deal, and even politicians at election time, have been known to visit the pool. However, few endanger themselves by bathing in the actual pool; there are shower cubicles carrying water pumped from the sacred source, and it's possible to take sacred water away to continue the rituals at home.

The pools are looked after by a guardian family, a responsibility passed down through the generations. Though they are not allowed to profit from their role for fear of upsetting the spirits, donations are gratefully accepted.

The life cycle of the crocodile

The Nile crocodile (*Crocodylus niloticus*) is the top predator in Gambian waters. These flesh-eating reptiles are supremely adapted to their environment, having changed little, evolutionarily speaking, for over 65 million years.

Environment

Nile crocodiles are at home in rivers and estuaries. Their noses and eyes sit at the very top of the head, allowing them to watch the banks while much of their body is submerged. For swimming and diving they have ears that close when submerged, clear third eyelids that cover the pupils, allowing them to see underwater, a muscular tail, webbed toes and short, powerful limbs for speed.

Crocodiles spend many hours basking in the sun on sandy banks and tidal flats. This increases the body temperature and improves digestion. Adult crocodiles can reduce their metabolic rate and heartbeat, often remaining inactive for much of the day.

Diet

Young crocs feed on insects, frogs and small fish. For adult crocodiles, larger fish make up the bulk of their diet, though they do take warthog, bushbuck and other deer, waiting motionless in the water and making high-speed surprise attacks when the animals come to drink. Despite their impressive teeth, they cannot chew; those gnashers are for grabbing and holding. They simply swallow whole chunks of food, which are processed in the stomach. It was assumed that crocodiles required a lot of food, but research has shown that they have a very slow metabolism and a large meal can satisfy one for weeks. However, they can eat up to half their immense body weight at one sitting.

Reproduction

A large male will fight rivals to gain control of a stretch of river and will have a harem of females. Mating takes place in November and December and there is a three-month incubation period. Nests comprising large mounds of vegetable matter are built above high-tide mark on the riverbanks. The female lays around 50 eggs and covers them so that the temperature remains constant.

The exact temperature decides the sex of the whole batch of eggs – if it falls below 31.7°C (89°F) or rises above 34.5°C (94°F), then the eggs will develop female young. Between

You can get quite close to these creatures, but be careful!

these temperatures they will develop into males.

The mother protects the nest with great vigour. When the young start to hatch they call to her, stimulating her to dig them out and take them to the water. She stays with her hatchlings for the first few weeks. The eggs and young hatchlings suffer the most attrition in the whole crocodile life cycle. Eggs are taken by predators, and young hatchlings (about 25cm/10in in length) make a perfect meal for large river fish, plus numerous bird species. Less than 5 per cent of eggs hatch and reach maturity.

Growth and lifespan
Young crocs grow at about 30cm (12in) per year. Sexual maturity happens in both sexes at about ten years of age. Adults found in The Gambia are not particularly large, usually under 4m (13ft), but examples across the continent have reached 6m (20ft) in length. The lifespan of the creatures has not been well documented; however, it's thought that they can live for up to 100 years.

Kololi

The Gambia's most concentrated tourist development lies on the coast west of Kololi village. It can be most neatly explained as one development along the road leading to the coast from the main road (Bertil Harding Highway) at the Palma Rima Resort, and a parallel development along the road leading from the main road to the Senegambia Hotel, known affectionately by everyone as the **Senegambia Strip**.

The 'strip' is little more than 300m (330yds) in length, but it's a great place for a beer and some passable food at one of 20 or so eateries. There's also an ATM here, though you might need to prompt the bank staff to fill it up with cash before you can use it. It's possible to walk between the two areas, but taxis are cheap, plentiful and more sensible after dark when there is no street lighting.

Kotu

Set around the outlet of the Kotu Stream, Kotu resort is little more than a handful of hotels, the best of which is the Kombo Beach, and restaurants backed up by a small craft market. However, it has arguably the best stretch of sand on the tourist coast and it's less high-paced than the Senegambia Strip in Kololi (*see above*). There is some excellent birdwatching on the doorstep around the river's edge. Where the main road crosses the river there's a hut where you can hire a government-approved guide, while unofficial 'bumster' guides (*see pp16–17*) will appear from behind every bush. An impressive pair of binoculars doesn't necessarily make a good guide; ask to see an identity card!

Makasutu Culture Forest

One of The Gambia's first forays into ecotourism and now receiving international acclaim, Makasutu is a unique project that couldn't have come to fruition without the efforts and enthusiasm of two Englishmen, James English and Laurence Williams. The two bought a small tract of gallery forest beside Mandina Bolong in 1992 and by 1999 owned 4sq km (1^{1}/$_{2}$sq miles). Initially they simply wanted to create a small travellers' motel. Today there's an award-winning lodge, a welcome centre, a nature trail and boat

A baboon in Makasutu Culture Forest

Kotu beach is perfect for sun-worshipping

trips on the *bolong* – perfect for birdwatchers – and the most comprehensive information about bird and animal species to be found anywhere in the country. The native wildlife has been left undisturbed to the extent that the troop of baboons that inhabit the forest may take it upon themselves to join you for lunch, wreaking havoc by raiding the rubbish bins and stealing bananas from plates, all to the great delight of the guests.

There's a much more serious side to Makasutu, however. The forest is invaluable as a habitat of ancient virgin forest with a rich biodiversity. English and Williams wanted to preserve and document this, yet also to make it a valuable resource for the community. To this end they employ dozens of local people as guides, restaurant staff and cooks; they have also worked tirelessly to promote the **Makasutu Wildlife Trust**, which, among other aims, encourages local education in biodiversity at Gambian schools. The trust is fostering links with international organisations including the Eden Project in the UK.

A tour of the forest brings you into contact with many valuable plants used by generations of Gambians for house construction, boatbuilding or natural medicines. You can visit a genuine traditional herbalist and fortune-teller, a much-revered member of traditional Gambian society, who will predict what your future has in store.

The Makasutu evening spectacular is a magical experience, with tribal dancers landing from a dugout canoe by the light of the stars and flaming torches. To the sound of tribal drums the tempo rises to a frenzy of movement around a huge campfire, with *kankurangs* and *kumpos* (spirit guides) adding to the excitement.

In late 2006, Makasutu reached agreement with ten surrounding communities to expand these original programmes into one of the largest and most innovative sustainable tourism projects in Africa.
Mandina Ba. Tel: 774 3322. www.makasutu.com. Open: daily 8am–5pm. Sat evening cultural spectacular from 8pm (must be pre-booked). Admission charge.

Serrekunda

When Bathurst reached a certain size it could not expand any further because of the restrictive Tanbi Wetlands Complex mangrove swamps that

THE LEGEND OF MAKASUTU

When English and Williams first discovered this land it had not been settled or farmed for centuries. Makasutu means 'sacred and deep forest' in Mandinka, and a local legend stated that the head of an illustrious tribal leader had been buried here after he was slain in battle, his spirit protected by *djinns* who drive away any prospective settler.

The pair were undeterred by the legend, vowing to preserve the essence of the place, and the spirits seem happy with what's been achieved. It was only after the eco-attraction came to fruition that they heard of another Mandinka legend – that of two white men who would come to save the forest and make it famous!

blocked its landward boundaries. Gambians looked for a location to create a satellite community and found it to the west, inland from the coast at Serrekunda, then a minuscule and insignificant farming village. Today, whereas Banjul can claim to be the capital and perhaps the brains of The Gambia, Serrekunda is certainly the country's heart. Over 20 per cent of the population live here and the place pulses with energy at all times of the day. Every morning before dawn many thousands of people stream out of Serrekunda to work in Banjul or the Kombo resorts. Your tour guide or your waiting staff will probably live here, as do the bulk of the government civil service.

Serrekunda is not exactly a town or a city. As with many things in The Gambia, the urban area simply grew organically, and several extended

Pirogue trip on Mandina Bolong

'villages' are now glued together in a seemingly endless maze of dirt streets and alleyways where thousands of family compounds stand cheek by jowl, intersected by major thoroughfares that funnel cars into a never-ending traffic jam of inefficient exhausts and old diesel engines.

The town has no museums or other real tourist attractions – it's the sheer weight of human existence that makes it a must for all visitors who want to understand what really makes this country tick. This atmosphere is most palpable at the daily market – the largest in the country – where fish, fowl and kilos of seasonal vegetables are bartered for, bought and sold. It's much less a tourist attraction than Albert Market in Banjul (*see pp33–4*), and foreign visitors may be bowled over by the scale of the

place and the merchandise on offer, be it a replacement aluminium cooking pot, a goat or a hand-stitched linen shirt. There's a small craft area at the heart of the market where prices (negotiable) are lower than in the capital.
Market on corner of Mosque Road and Sayer Jobe Avenue. Open: daily 8am–7pm (some stalls close 1pm Fri).

Tanje

Tanje (also spelt Tangeh and Tanji) sits on the coast at the current southern boundary of the tourist strip. The **Sheraton Resort** is only a couple of kilometres to the north, which will definitely change the atmosphere in the village in the next few years. Until then, Tanje is a touch of reality, in contrast to the settlement of Kololi where tourism overshadows everything else.

Serrekunda and the tourist coast

The sandy beach at Tanje

Fish drying in the sun, Tanje

The **Fish Market** on the waterfront in the heart of the settlement is the largest in The Gambia. Several rows of permanent open-fronted counters are supplemented by impromptu beach stalls where the ladies drive a hard bargain to get the best price. As in the rest of the world, fish is becoming an expensive option, but you can't get fresher than this as catches are landed throughout the day. While it's the men who do the fishing on their 8- to 10-man pirogues, casting their nets and lines by hand, the heavily laden baskets and buckets are unloaded by hand by slender girls no older than 18.

North of the village centre is **Tanje River Bird Reserve**, a 6sq km (2sq mile) tract of land bounding the Tanje River which was The Gambia's first dedicated bird reserve. The beauty for

'twitchers' is that in this seemingly small area there's a whole range of habitats, from mangrove swamps and tidal flats to coastal woodland and sand dunes, so it attracts a vast range of birds, both native and migratory. Included in the reserve are the **Bijol Islands**, the country's only offshore territory, where seabirds and turtles nest undisturbed by predators. Unlike Abuko, there's no trail here so access is much more difficult – which is good news for the birds.

Tanje Village Museum is a private enterprise set up by the man who was once curator of the National Museum of The Gambia in Banjul. His brainchild was to create a living museum of Gambian lifestyle so that visitors could see how the people lived and find out more about their habits and customs. 'Putting The Gambia under one roof' was how he succinctly phrased it. The small village re-creates a family compound – the kind you'll see thousands of if you travel 'upcountry' to the interior of The Gambia. You'll also be able to watch the weaver and the blacksmith at work, examples of small-scale craftsmanship that are both still thriving industries. The small on-site museum has several rooms with information about native flora and fauna, created in conjunction with the Parks and Wildlife Management Service of The Gambia. Most interesting are the cases showing indigenous plants and their uses. Further rooms feature traditional musical instruments.

You'll also find the **Camel Safari** headquarters at Tanje. You'll need to book as part of an organised tour, but the stately cruise down Tanje's beach atop this ship of the desert is a great experience.

Tanje River Bird Reserve. Open: daily 8am–dusk. Donation expected.
Tanje Village Museum. Tel: 926 618. Open: daily 9am–5pm. Admission charge.
Camel Safari. Tel: 446 1083. Book direct or through a tour operator.

Time for tea at the Tanje Village Museum

Birdlife of The Gambia

Without doubt The Gambia is one of the world's best destinations for birdwatchers. Geographically it sits in a perfect location for migrant species that make the long journey from Europe to South Africa in the European winter (returning north again for the summer), and the wide range of habitats it holds – from salt-estuary to riverine to woodland – attracts many different types of birds.

The Gambia's national parks protect healthy areas of pristine landscape well away from the interference of modern human activity, but you'll be surprised just how many species you'll be able to spot even if you don't leave the 'tourist coast'. Take an early-morning boat trip in the Tanbi Wetlands Complex (*see pp40–41*) to listen to the birdsong at dawn, or book time in a hide at Abuko Nature Reserve (*see pp60–61*). Tanje River Bird Reserve (*see p56*) offers a wealth of options, while the Kotu Stream is a great place for waterbirds. The areas of wasteland between hotel blocks can be a surprising source of birdlife, from hummingbirds to vultures, and herons and egrets can be spotted just about everywhere.

If you have an interest in birdwatching, you can book a specialised tour and hire a guide who'll be able to lead you to some rare and extraordinary birds (*see p157*). Scientists have documented over 500 species, and species counts of 250–300 are not unusual for the amateur during an average week here in the European winter.

What to spot

Here is just a handful of species you may spot during a holiday in The Gambia.

A long-tailed glossy starling

Wetland species

African darter – a cormorant-like bird, sometimes called the 'snakebird' because it has a long neck.

Whimbrel – the noisiest bird in The Gambia. The most widespread of the curlew family, it overwinters here in large numbers.

Pied kingfisher – a small, noisy bird with black-and-white plumage, it is numerous in *bolongs*.

Giant kingfisher – the largest kingfisher in Africa at over 40cm (16in) in height.

Pink-backed pelican – an African native species.

Western Reef heron – found in all wetland areas.

Goliath heron – the world's largest heron, sometimes standing over 1.4m (4½ft) in height.

A great egret from the savanna

Freshwater river species

Blue-cheeked bee-eater – an overwintering species that adds spectacular colour to the sky.

Egyptian plover – also called the 'crocodile bird' because it can be seen cleaning decaying meat from around the teeth of these giant reptiles.

Senegal thick-knee – a resident breeding wader with large yellow eyes.

Savanna species

Beautiful sunbird – it's a delightful name, and this multicoloured bird can be found in hotel grounds.

Purple glossy starling – resident breeder and a numerous, gregarious bird.

Western grey plantain-eater – feeds on a range of fruits and seeds.

Abyssinian roller – brilliant plumage and around 30cm (12in) in height, these are insect feeders.

Palm-nut vulture – whose favourite food is not flesh, but the seed of the palm-nut tree.

Hooded vulture – a large scavenger often found by rubbish tips.

Great egret – largest of the species.

Walk: Abuko Nature Reserve

Abuko Nature Reserve, an exceptional tract of protected forest at the head of Lamin Bolong, offers one of the easiest locations to spot a range of wildlife (see pp43–5). Try to visit early in the morning or late in the afternoon, when the animals are more active. The path around the park is measured by regular markers counting up to 107. It's simple to follow and there are plenty of rest stops along the way. You will find the services of a guide useful in identifying trees, birds and other animals.

Allow 2 hours, or longer depending on wildlife-watching opportunities.
Distance: 2.5km (1¹/₂ miles).

Once you enter the park, the forest closes in around the dusty track. About 200m (220yds) from the start of the walk you'll cross a river bed on a narrow bridge.

1 River bed

This river bed acts as a conduit during the rainy season, filling waterholes that provide the park with fresh water year-round.
Another 100m (110yds) or so along the trail you'll catch your first sight of the watering hole, and then the Darwin Field Station on the right.

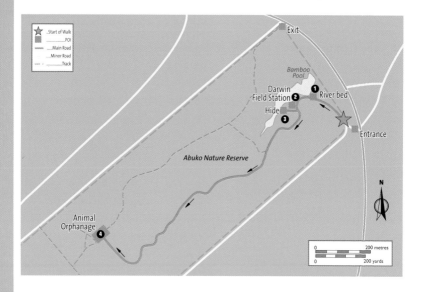

Start of Walk
POI
Main Road
Minor Road
Track

Exit

Bamboo Pool

Darwin Field Station ❷

River bed ❶

Hide
❸

Entrance

Abuko Nature Reserve

N

Animal Orphanage
❹

0   200 metres
0   200 yards

2 Darwin Field Station

This acts as a base for field scientists but it also provides excellent information for visitors. Climb to the observation deck for panoramic views across the watering hole where, at most times of day, you can spot crocodiles basking, plus a selection of wading birds. Perhaps if you are lucky a deer will come down to drink or a monitor lizard might crawl through the undergrowth.

Just around the corner from the research station is a short route right to a hide at the water's edge.

3 Hide

This hide provides a close-up view of the animals and birds that frequent the

A shy deer may cross your path

park. It's available for hire and is often used by birding groups. The best time to install yourself is before sunrise.

From here, it's a straightforward walk into the heart of the dense forest.
At distance post 29 there is a shortcut path to the exit if you are already feeling jaded, but otherwise continue on. Marker 65 marks the furthest reach of the park and here you'll find the Animal Orphanage.

4 Animal Orphanage

This is a strange collection of animals in large but not particularly therapeutic cages. Most surprising are the hyenas with their impressive musculature. Another cage has a collection of baboons rescued from homes in The Gambia. Don't get close because some have developed very antisocial habits.

You'll also find a refreshment stall here with water and other cold drinks, plus a couple of craft stalls.

Leave the orphanage on the lane that runs to the right of the baboon compound. From here it's approximately 1.25km ($^3/4$ mile) to the exit, where you'll find a small craft market. Or, if you've left a vehicle at the entrance car park, take the footpath right at marker 95, which leads back to the ticket office.

Animals en route

Along the way you should encounter monkeys grubbing for roots or hiding in the undergrowth on either flank. You may also be lucky enough to see a duiker (deer) or a mongoose, both of which are more wary of humans.

Tour: The highlights of the tourist coast

The highlights of The Gambia's tourist coast are many – more than you could fit into one day. The attractions detailed here offer a varied itinerary with time to relax, shop and shake hands with one of nature's wildest creatures.

Allow 8 hours.

Distance: 58km (36 miles).

From the hotel strip at Senegambia, head north along Bertil Harding Highway to Bakau. Turn left at Kairaba Avenue and right on Garba Jahumpa Road for 1km (¹/₂ mile) until you reach Sait Matty Road. Once there, you'll need to ask for exact directions to Katchikally

Crocodile Pool because it sits in a maze of dusty lanes and isn't signposted.

1 Katchikally Crocodile Pool

Katchikally is the most accessible of several sacred crocodile pools that are still used by local people in animist ceremonies (*see p49*). Tourists get to pet the somnolent beasts and have their photographs taken.

From Katchikally, ask for directions back to Sait Matty Road and return down Garba Jahumpa Road to Kairaba Avenue. Turn left onto this long arterial thoroughfare and continue on until it meets Mosque Road. Turn right here, and at the end of the road (after 1.5km/1 mile) you'll find Serrekunda Market on your left.

2 Serrekunda market

Serrekunda Market (*see p55*) is the region's most interesting, in-your-face, African experience. Visit whether you want to buy or not.

From the crossroads where Mosque Road meets Sayer Jobe Avenue, take a left and

head south towards Sukuta and Brufut.
After 4km (2¹/2 miles) the road splits.
Take the right fork and continue for
another 7km (4¹/2 miles), meeting the
coast at Tanje. Once past the fish market
you'll see a small sign for Tanje Village
Museum on the left.

3 Tanje Village Museum

Tanje Village Museum (see pp56–7)
offers 'The Gambia in one spot', re-
creating a typical upcountry village.
The guides are helpful and
knowledgeable.
From Tanje carry on south until you
reach Sanyang (10km/6 miles). Turn right
on the second main dirt track in the
village and head to the end of the road.
Rainbow Beach Bar is on the left after the
fishing station.

4 Rainbow Beach Bar

This large and pleasant bar (open: daily)
is situated on a wonderful beach, and
is a popular stopping point for tours.
The owner, Jowla, is very friendly
and enterprising.
Return to Sanyang village and take the
road east in the direction of Jambanjeli
and Brikama. When the road reaches
the crossroads at Brikama after 9km
(5¹/2 miles), turn left and 300m (330yds)
along on the left is the craft market.

5 Brikama craft market

Brikama craft market (see p46) is the
best place to shop for wooden carvings.
The articles are carved here so the
range is very good and the prices keen.

From Brikama, head north along the
main road towards Banjul. When you
reach the airport (after approximately
7km/4¹/2 miles), take the left turn for the
resorts and continue for 6.5km (4 miles)
until you reach the small sign for Kombo
Distillery on the left. Turn down the
dusty track.

6 Kim Kombo Plantation
and Distillery

One of the recent successes of the
eco-industry that has sprung up in
recent years, the distillery is a British
enterprise, a 10ha (25-acre) fruit
plantation that produces a range of
excellent liqueurs. You'll be invited to a
generous tasting session. The distillery
also holds an African evening twice a
week (www.kimkombo.gm).
Return to the main road and turn left;
cross the intersection and you'll return to
the Senegambia Strip in a few minutes.

A display of liqueurs at Kim Kombo Distillery

The north shore

Separated from Banjul by the expansive waters of the River Gambia, the north shore offers a contrasting lifestyle that's easy to explore on a day trip from the coastal resorts. Some of The Gambia's most famous tourist attractions lie in this region and it's the centre of the slave heritage trail, which offers an emotional symbolic homecoming for many African Americans.

Getting to the north shore is an adventure in itself. The Banjul–Barra commercial ferry crossing is a full-on slice of the push and pull of the daily grind African style, where modern 4WD vehicles vie for space with donkey carts, and foot passengers always carry more baggage than they can possibly handle. Crossing by vehicle requires a wait of at least two hours at any time of day. If you are touring independently it's much less time-consuming to take a taxi to the ferry at Banjul, travel across as a foot passenger and then contract another taxi in Barra to reach the attractions. If you do cross by vehicle, for safety reasons don't sit in your car seat during the crossing. Once there, road conditions vary from excellent to terrible, but you can also reach many north-shore attractions by boat – a more relaxing alternative to road travel.

Albreda

The slave trade along the River Gambia was an international affair. Until the 1850s, the French administered their operation from Albreda on the north bank, not far from Juffureh (*see pp74–5*) and the English headquarters at San Domingo (*see pp78–9*) and James Island (*see pp68–71*) – one small anomaly of European international relations in that most complicated of centuries. Today the village is the landing site for boat trips on the *Roots Heritage Trail*, and visitors will make their way along the jetty to a re-creation of the 'Freedom Flagpole', so called because if a slave could break free and touch the flagpole he would be freed. No records exist to show how many actually managed this, but there were instructions that any such prisoner would have to be branded with a distinguishing mark so that if they were ever captured again, there was proof that they could not be taken into bondage.

The small garden around the freedom pole has informative displays about the origins of slavery and about the historical remains hereabouts.

Gambians are not proud of the fact that there was a slave caste within their own society before the arrival of Europeans, and it was partly this acceptance of the concept of slavery by Africans themselves that allowed the colonialists to begin the trade that would lead to grotesque exploitation on an unimaginable scale.

Looking out to the river from the Freedom Flagpole, you'll see ruined buildings to the left along the foreshore, now surrounded by a fleet of colourful dugout pirogues. Locals may tell you that it's a slave warehouse, but it's actually the CFAO trade warehouse dating from much later, in the post-slavery era.

Bao Bolong Wetland Reserve

The Gambia's largest protected area, the Bao Bolong (also spelled Bao Bolon) Wetland Reserve covers over 230sq km (89sq miles) on and around the Bao Bolong and a handful of other tributaries of the River Gambia flowing into it from the north. There's no permanent human settlement along the water's edge, leaving the area a pristine environment for native wildlife. The shoreline offers a wall of mangrove standing up to 12m (39ft) high in places, where some of The Gambia's few remaining manatees (sea cows) are said to forage, along with an equally small population of hippos and more numerous crocodiles and clawless otters. North of the mangroves lie vast marshland and tidal flats, ideal

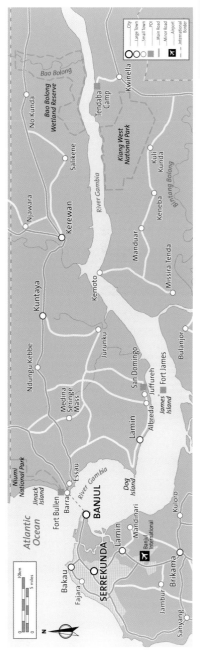

The wetlands of the Bao Bolong Reserve

for wading birds, while just inland from here is a sharp escarpment leading to tracts of dry savanna

THE RAMSAR INTERNATIONAL WETLANDS CONVENTION

Wetland environments have long been viewed as some of the most threatened in the world as river systems are 'managed' and land drained and claimed for farming. Ratified in Ramsar, Iran in 1971, the Wetlands Convention is a treaty of commitment to preserve wetland environments and provides governments with a framework for action within their own country while setting up an international forum of good practice, giving environmentalists access to expert advice. Over 1,600 wetlands have been listed as worthy of protection worldwide, covering over 145 million ha (358 million acres) in area (*www.ramsar.org*).

woodland. This is one of West Africa's richest bird environments, including occasional sightings of Pel's fishing-owl and brown-necked parrots, and numerous African darters, goliath and western reef herons and impressive African fish eagles. The reserve has been included as a site of importance by the Ramsar International Wetlands Convention (*see box*) and in mid-2006 a bird viewing platform was opened, built with funding from the West African Bird Study Association (WABSA).

The park headquarters are situated at Dai Mandinka, south of the main highway and accessed from it via the village of No Kunda. Since there are no park maps or well-signposted trails, you are best advised to take a guide from here to make inroads into the savanna, where a handful of rural villages still consist of traditional round huts, or you can rent a dugout canoe to explore the *bolongs*.

Alternatively, you can access the reserve from the south bank of the River Gambia at Tendaba Camp (*see p90*). Although this won't allow you to step ashore and see the inland environments of Bao Bolong, it's an excellent way to explore the mangrove and wetland scenery and its associated birds and animals.

100km (62 miles) upriver from the mouth of the River Gambia. Open: daily 8am–6pm. Admission charge.

Barra

This tiny bustling town is the northern docking point for the Banjul ferry, with foot and vehicle traffic feeding the local economy. With car traffic queuing for at least five hours, and commercial traffic often waiting a week to cross, Barra makes a living catering to its huge temporary population at inexpensive street stalls and selling everything a Senegalese truck driver might need while he keeps a patient vigil before his turn to cross comes. The main approaches to the ferry dock are crammed with stationary traffic waited on by hundreds of youngsters offering

The River Gambia at Barra Point

peeled oranges, cashews and peanuts, and fresh water or fruit juice in single-portion plastic bags.

If you arrive in Barra as a foot passenger your exit from the port takes you through the town market. This is much more workaday than Albert Market in Banjul (*see pp33–4*) but offers a fascinating picture of the kinds of merchandise that Gambians and Senegalese on the move count as necessities, including vast quantities of plastic razors, jellybean sandals and small teapots used to brew up Gambian style (*see p18*).

Fort Bullen

The docking station at Barra Point is still protected by the sturdy bulk of Fort Bullen, built by the British as a counterpoint to the fort at Bathurst during the early 19th century in order to block French and Portuguese slave-running in the years after it had been abolished in British territories. Still complete with its round corner turrets, it saw service again in World War II – the remains of an anti-aircraft gunning placement that was installed at the time can still be seen – and sometimes plays host to Gambian army manoeuvres today. The huge river navigation beacon installed in the inner courtyard does somewhat spoil the atmosphere, but there are excellent views of the channel from the battlements.

Open: Mon–Sat 9am–7pm.
Admission charge.

DOG ISLAND

When the Portuguese first began exploring the river in the 15th century, they heard the loud barking of what sounded like huge dogs emanating from this small islet close to the north shore. Though a little frightened at the thought of coming face to face with vicious carnivores, they made landfall to find that instead of dogs, the call was in fact the warning sound made by baboons who felt threatened by their approach. However, the name Dog Island remains to this day.

James Island

There are few pieces of land on earth so intimately connected with the slave trade as this islet, once known as St Andrew's Island, replete with baobabs in the middle of the River Gambia. Between 1651, when it was founded by the Duke of Courland, and 1829, when its fort was abandoned, Africans were packed like sardines into the holds of cargo vessels and shipped to the Americas to work as slaves on the plantations. Between 1731 and 1740 over 26,000 slaves were documented as having been 'exported', but estimates suggest that hundreds of thousands met this same fate, their last view of their homeland being the soil of James Island. Most would never see Africa again.

Even if the historical era holds little interest for the visitor, it's hard not to feel the human story as you clamber onto the rickety wooden jetty to reach the island. The river is so wide here that it's difficult to see either bank. It must have instilled utter despair in the prisoners knowing it was almost

The fort, James Island

Looking out through Fort James' ruined battlements

impossible to escape and that their fate was sealed. The island is extremely small but was six times larger in 1651, the area having been eaten away by the force of the tides in the intervening centuries. Slaves were transported here from the north shore and kept in cramped cells for two weeks before finally being loaded on board.

The fort had 35 dungeons, each with a capacity of 25 slaves, so maximum capacity was 875 individuals. The two-week interval between arrival and departure was usually enough to cause the weakest ones to die, which meant they didn't take up ship space that could be devoted to a stronger specimen.

In addition to its job as a slave warehouse, the fort had an important defensive role and was constantly harried by the French, who also controlled tribal lands in the Senegambia region. They took the fort in 1695, 1702 and again in 1704, but each time it returned to British control. In 1719 the fort was seized by pirates and in 1768 it was attacked by Niumi forces, tribespeople who controlled the north bank around what is now Barra (*see pp67–8*). One can feel a certain sympathy for the soldiers garrisoned here, so far away from home and any semblance of normal society, and

indeed the company did mutiny in 1708 when morale must have been at rock bottom.

Today only the ruined walls of the main central structure remain. There's one slave cell and a few sections of curtain wall, but the island requires extreme intervention if it is not to be lost completely in the next few years. UNESCO have added James Island to their World Heritage Site list, and one hopes that this will help to secure some kind of international assistance.
Access by boat from Banjul or Albreda.
Open: daily 8am–6pm.
Admission charge.

Replica slave bracelets on display at James Island

The colonial slave trade

A severe shortage of labour in the New World was the initial catalyst for the slave trade. The indigenous people of the Caribbean and South America had been swiftly wiped out by cruelty and disease, and the cash crop systems that made the colonies profitable needed large numbers of strong farmhands. Arab traders and African tribal leaders in Western Africa were selling men, women and children and the colonists made the decision to buy.

Monument outside the Slavery Museum in Juffureh

The first slaves were reported in the New World in 1502, with numbers reaching a peak in the 1840s. At the height of the system, thousands of Africans were being shipped every month. Definitive numbers are unknown, but the minimum agreed by scholars is ten million individuals. Almost 6 per cent are thought to have been despatched from the region of Senegambia (Gambia, Senegal, Guinea-Bissau and Guinea). The journey was a brutal one. Captains expected that at least 25 per cent of their human cargo would die during the crossing.

The 'triangular trade'

A well-plied route linked slave countries, colonies and European ports. The three-leg journey became known as the 'triangular trade'.

Boats departed south from Europe to Africa carrying bartering beads, cloth, weapons and rum. When they reached The Gambia, captains would sell or barter these for slaves. Once the hulls were packed with this human cargo the ships departed on the ten-week transatlantic crossing to America and the Caribbean – the Middle Passage – where the Africans would be sold into slavery at markets

A mural depicting slaves

Abolition

The slave trade was abolished in the British Empire in 1807, but this related to the taking of any new slaves, not to the owning of any existing ones. Ironically, after the British abolished slavery, the trade expanded as the French and Portuguese fed demand via a 'black market'. In The Gambia it was necessary to build a fort at Bathurst, now Banjul (see pp32–9), and Fort Bullen (see p68) at the mouth of the River Gambia, to stop foreign ships travelling upriver to take Africans from under the very noses of the British. The owning of slaves finally became illegal in the British Empire in 1834. In The Gambia, McCarthy Island was declared a refuge for freed slaves and a number returned to Africa to begin a new life on their native soil.

in the port. This freed up cash to be spent on fresh cargoes of rum, molasses and sugar – later cotton and tobacco – to be transported back to Europe.

The appeal of the triangular trade system for boat owners was that they could make massive profits on each leg of the journey, not having to wait until the ships finally reached home-port again. Because of the possibility of one single ship sinking, or being lost to pirates or an enemy, it was normal for investors to have part shares in many ships, thus spreading the financial risk.

Effects on Africa – food for thought

British adventurer Archibald Dalzel (1740–1811), who served as governor of Ouidah, Benin, suggested that Africa could cope well enough with the losses of several generations of healthy men and women, whereas Walter Rodney (1942–80), a Guyanese historian, claimed that slavery is directly responsible for Africa being underdeveloped to the modern day. This is a question to ponder as African nations demand an apology from their former colonial overlords.

Juffureh

This tiny village was an insignificant farming settlement until 1976. Today it's one of the most famous locations in Africa, courtesy of *Roots: The Saga of an American Family*, a book that galvanised African American society and put The Gambia on the international map (*see pp76–7*).

When Alex Haley named Juffureh as the native village of his ancestor Kunta Kinte, the first of his line to be sold into slavery in America, the family and village had little idea of the attention it would receive. Juffureh sits only a few minutes' walk inland from Albreda (*see pp64–5*), with James Island (*see pp68–71*) only a short boat trip offshore, so it has always lain close to the story of slavery. But before very long hundreds of people, many of them African Americans searching for their own family roots, began to arrive to walk the dusty paths in Kunta Kinte's footsteps. Today visitors of all creeds and colours are still coming.

The Kinte family still reside here, though the mud and straw huts they lived in have been replaced by brick compounds. The knowledgeable official guides have plenty of background information about the slave trade in general and the Kinte family tree. The matriarch of the family takes time to sit with visitors, answering questions through an interpreter. You can also purchase an informative booklet explaining the background to the book with biographical details about Haley and the impact of the book on the African American population in the USA.

The Slavery Museum at Juffureh – officially the **National Museum of the North Bank** – does a far better job than its Banjul counterpart, and there's a wealth of information about this inhumane trade, why it happened and how the whole system worked. Housed in Maurel Freres Building, a trading post built in 1840, the information is presented in a straightforward manner, never leaning towards the judgemental; in a way this only adds to the impact on visitors as the full horror of what took place on 'the voyage of no return' begins to sink in. The rusting manacles, yokes and chains show the brutal treatment meted out to the captives, while official documents listing totals 'exported' and numbers dying before transportation or during the voyage make very sombre reading. There's a model of the fort on James Island as it looked in its heyday, which needs to be held in the memory when you set eyes on what now remains.

The final gallery in the museum has a more uplifting, emancipatory message. Entitled 'Portraits of a New Generation', it features photographs and short biographies of African Americans who have thrived in the USA and without whose contribution modern America would be a much poorer place (not only financially but also spiritually and morally). Positive stories of influential politicians such as Condoleezza Rice (former American Secretary of State) and Marc Morial (former Mayor of New Orleans), musicians such as Queen Latifah and Wynton Marsalis, plus a hundred or more sportspeople, businesspeople and scientists, are highlighted, showing the rich talent bequeathed to the nation by the generations of slave men and women who arrived powerless on American shores.

Kinte Family Compound. Open: daily 8am–6pm. Donation expected for any photographs taken.

National Museum of the North Bank. Tel: 422 6244. Open: Mon–Thur 10am–5pm, Fri 10am–1pm. Admission charge.

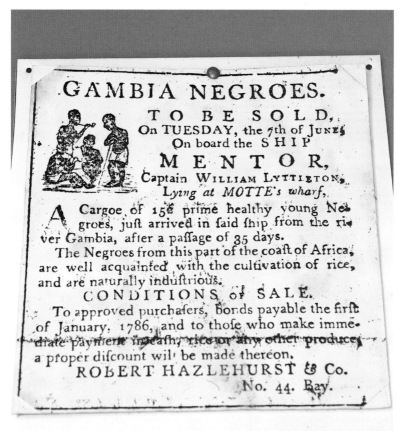

A poster exhibit at the Slavery Museum, Juffureh

The *Roots* phenomenon

In 1976 the publication of *Roots: The Saga of an American Family* captured the imagination of a generation of African Americans. The story of Mandinka warrior Kunta Kinte, kidnapped from Gambia in 1767 and sold into slavery in the USA, and the subsequent generations of the Kinte family – all ancestors of the book's author Alex Haley – showed African Americans that their history was not an anonymous one. The novel was an instant hit in the USA and was subsequently published worldwide in 37 languages. A TV mini-series screened in 1977 was avidly watched by 130 million viewers.

Roots prompted many African Americans to undertake detailed research into their own genealogy, but just as importantly the journey from the United States to The Gambia made by Haley became a pilgrimage undertaken by many more from all tribal backgrounds. The Kinte clan became symbolic kin of millions of American tribal descendants, and a trip to tiny Juffureh became an emotional homecoming.

Recently, doubts have been thrown on whether this tiny village is exactly the ancestral home of a man named Kunta Kinte. Several authors have pored over Haley's research and found fault with the dates and locations. Some have even suggested that the *griot* (*see p22*) Haley came to see at Juffureh in the early 1970s had been coached with answers that would please the visitor – little realising the chain of events that this would set in motion. But what is without doubt is that, even if Haley was mistaken, misdirected or deceitful, the power of the *Roots* story is in no way diminished.

Alex Haley in his US Coastguard days

Entrance to the Roots Heritage Trail (*see p75*)

Alex Haley

Alex Haley was born in Ithaca, New York in 1921, and his family moved south when he was a child. In 1939 he joined the US Coastguard. During long voyages he would alleviate the fear and boredom by writing stories and discovered he had a talent for it. After World War II, Haley transferred to the journalist division of the Coastguard where he worked until he earned his retirement in 1959. He then began a new career, writing full time.

Haley's first significant piece appeared in *Playboy* in 1962 when he interviewed legendary jazz musician Miles Davis about, among other things, his attitude to racism. This led to an ongoing theme throughout the 1960s where Haley would interview leading African Americans, including Dr Martin Luther King and the boxer Muhammad Ali. In 1963 Haley interviewed African American human rights activist Malcolm X and this meeting led to Haley being asked to ghostwrite Malcolm X's autobiography. The resulting tome was said by *Time Magazine* to be one of the most important non-fiction books of the 20th century.

In 1966 Haley began research on a more personal story, the search for his 'roots'. This journey led him through several generations to Annapolis, Maryland, site of Kunta Kinte's arrival on American soil, then across the Atlantic to Juffureh, from where his family were said to originate. He won the Pulitzer Prize for his efforts.

Haley was working on a second genealogical novel, *Queen*, when he died of a heart attack in 1992. At his request the story was completed by David Stevens, an American actor.

Niumi National Park

Named after the Niumi peoples who traditionally occupied this region and the government district of Niumi that administrates the area, Niumi National Park protects coastal wetland environments that stretch all the way up the northern Gambia coastline from just north of Fort Bullen (see p68) to the Senegal border. It's only a stone's throw from Banjul but it's a little-explored park, at the heart of which run the sinuous curves of Massarinko Bolong, a waterway that sees few people. There are no public transport services to the landward side and it's not yet been added to the overland tour-group itinerary.

Niumi is a favourite location for migrant birds with a high overall species count, but most don't spend much time here. It's a vital pit stop down the African coast and they take a few days to replenish fat stocks before carrying on north or south, depending on the season. However, there are plenty of native herons and ospreys, and the savanna forests are known for their warblers.

A few manatees are said to live in the waterways but you'll be very lucky to spot one; more frequent are dolphins, especially in the dry season. Niumi is also home to crocodiles and monitor lizards.

Jinack Island on the western boundary of the park is the most popular destination for day-trippers, but the name is misleading: it's only cut off from the rest of The Gambia by the width of a *bolong*. At low tide Jinack's beaches stretch for 10km (6 miles) and the interior of dry forest is ideal for birdwatching. Most of the island is in Gambian territory but the 'straight-as-a-die' border drawn up in colonial times cut off the upper point, which is now firmly Senegalese.
Northeast of Barra. Open: daily 8am–6pm. Admission charge.

San Domingo

Less then 1km (½ mile) from the centre of Juffureh, but little visited by modern tour groups, lie the remains of San Domingo, site of the first Portuguese settlement in Gambia, which was taken over by the British and served as the departure point for Fort James.

THE *ROOTS* TRAIL

One of the most popular day trips run by tour operators is the *Roots* Heritage Trail. This usually includes a lazy ferry trip from Banjul along the River Gambia with stops at Albreda, the National Museum of the North Bank (also known as the Slavery Museum), the Kinte family compound to meet the descendants of Alex Haley's ancestors (see pp76–7), then a visit to James Island before the boat comes back downriver to the capital. You'll take lunch on board and hopefully catch sight of the playful family of dolphins that live in the expanse of the saltwater estuary.

You'll be *toubab*-ed (see p20) from the moment you make landfall by children large and small, with pleading eyes asking for your empty plastic bottles (to carry drinking water to school), and hundreds of potential pen pals will seek to press scraps of paper with neatly printed names and addresses into your palm.

Here the slaves captured by African tribesmen would be handed over to the British in return for weapons and goods. As with many historical buildings on the Roots Trail, very little remains at San Domingo – merely one corner and buttress of the old British trading station – but it's worth treading the path from here to the river, the final few steps slaves would have taken on their native soil. The path leading to the ruins is surrounded by farmland and placid free-roaming cattle. You may catch sight of families of monkeys tearing through the undergrowth. *Open access.*

The ruins at San Domingo

Janjangbureh and the mid-river region

The mid-river region brings visitors face to face with The Gambia's true African roots. Hectares of dusty savanna form the country's arable heartland, with tiny thatched rural villages continuing ancient practices. The mid-river also introduces West Africa's mysterious past, startling evidence of a history never recorded but certainly sophisticated – a society that we may never fully understand.

As the River Gambia narrows the further inland you travel, so do the country's boundaries, sometimes extending only a few kilometres either side of the riverbanks. There are still only two crossing points east of the Banjul/Barra connection, and, although they share a common nationality, for the most part the north- and south-bank communities have little contact with each other.

The southern highway is in a diabolical condition. Asphalted by the British, it has seen little repair since the colonial era. Resurfacing and expansion are taking place at the western end but it will take at least five years to complete the whole route, even if today's pace is maintained. Most travellers take the easier north-coast road, which is a shame, as the lack of traffic makes the south-route settlements much more fascinating – you'll find children playing football on this supposedly arterial road, monkey families congregating for a spot of mutual preening, and snakes warming themselves on the last remaining patches of black tarmac in the early mornings. Completed up to Janjangbureh, the north-coast route is now smooth, fast asphalt, allowing you to speed on through but miss the rural life just outside the window.

At the moment these are your choices for trips upriver, for aside from occasional bespoke cruises (usually at the end of the tourist season and before the rains start – *see pp92–3*) there is absolutely no east/west river traffic to take you up to Janjangbureh.

Farafenni

This north-shore settlement is a constant hive of activity. It sits on the trans-Gambia highway close to the ferry crossing at Bambatenda/Yelitenda, and on a direct route with the Senegalese capital Dakar and its southern Casamance district. With the Gambian customs post in the heart of town it's a place where commercial traffic gets bottlenecked, so it's quite well stocked with eateries. It even has a couple of basic hotels if you want to break the journey upcountry, or spend some time at Bao Bolong Wetland Reserve (*see pp65–7*) to the west.

The town's *lumo* (country market) is one of the largest in The Gambia. Every Sunday the whole district travels to Farafenni to trade everything from cattle to machine parts at what turns into an open-air commercial jamboree. Those without mechanical horsepower arrive on the back of donkey- and horse-drawn carts, transformed into public transport for the day.

In addition to local fresh produce and livestock, you'll find traders from surrounding countries – French-speaking Malians, Guineans and Mauritanians – who sell all kinds of consumer goods including fabrics and clothing. You'll be able to explore and browse here without the pressure to buy that's sometimes felt at the tourist markets along the coast, though there are far fewer of the mass-produced souvenir items here. Try to time your visit for the *lumo* day (Sunday) if you can.

Janjangbureh (Georgetown)

Janjangbureh is a backwater in the modern Gambia, but for many years the town was a rival to Bathurst and the second city of the Gambia colony.

The town sits on mid-river McCarthy Island, leased from the local tribal chief

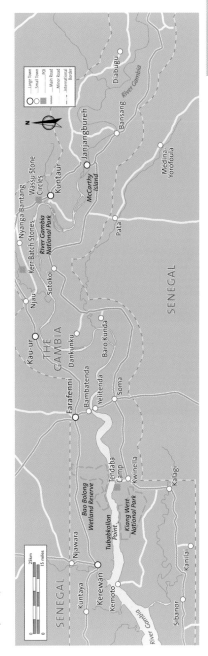

A ferry docks at Janjangbureh

by the British in 1823. They founded a fort and town named after the then monarch George IV. Capital of the Central River Division, the local people would have you believe that the history of Janjangbureh is as inextricably linked with colonial slavery as James Island (*see pp68–71*) and Juffureh (*see pp74–5*) in the west, closer to the river's mouth, but the story is a little more mundane. The town was founded after the British abolished slavery, and in many ways its raison d'être was to enforce that edict, not to defer it. The purpose of Georgetown was to protect the eastern boundaries of the British Gambia province from French troops in Senegal and to found a base from where

missionaries could spread the Christian word. In fact Wesleyan Protestants arrived here, founding their only church in West Africa (*see p95*). The island became a safe haven for freed slaves, the Akus, and those who escaped French and Portuguese incarceration. Farming was established and the fledgling settlement thrived.

Renamed Janjangbureh in 1995, the town is a full 300km (186 miles) upriver from Banjul. There's been very little investment in infrastructure since independence, and this is a world away from the busy and relatively cosmopolitan capital. Perhaps Janjangbureh feels slighted by the loss of its influence; one might even suggest that it succumbs to malaise, but that would be an injustice to the vibrant day-to-day activity that brings the streets to life.

Janjangbureh offers the most easterly crossing point of the River Gambia, but the ferries here cannot support any heavy goods traffic. The ferry on the north side can carry three or four vehicles, while the ferry on the south side is smaller and can carry only two vehicles. A new bridge to the south of the island was opened in July 2010.

Trade was one of the main industries in Georgetown. The north shores of the town still have the shells of immense late 18th-century and early 19th-century warehouses – the Maurel &

Prom building and the CFAO buildings that serviced the river traffic – and both would certainly make superb boutique hotels and restaurants for the modern tourist market, were the investment available. A local guide might sit you down with stories of how slaves were imprisoned in these sturdy structures, but these are too young to be slave warehouses. That is not to say, however, that before the founding of Georgetown the hunting and transporting of slaves didn't take place from these riverbanks; the trade was too insidious and widespread for it not to have happened, but it is necessary to state that these particular buildings played no part in it.

The Maurel & Prom building

One block inland from the wharf, the Commissioner's Office building betrays a style of 19th- and 20th-century utilitarian colonial architecture. The outposts of the British Empire didn't benefit from many architectural masterpieces and this building is devoid of any flourishes and frills.

The Wesleyans founded a mission school in Georgetown, which soon gained a reputation as the best in the Gambia colony. In 1927 it was renamed Armitage School and became the school of choice of the growing class of Gambian elite, with the motto 'Enter to Learn, Go Forward to Serve'. Immaculately uniformed boarders can still be found here, but the international schools in Banjul now offer serious competition.

In the heart of town is a small, well-tended park with a sapling baobab in the middle, which was planted to replace a mature, colonial-age one that was damaged in the 1990s. Known as the Freedom Tree, it is said that slaves who freed themselves from bondage and touched the baobab could not be transported to the Americas. Perhaps this tree, reminiscent of the flagpole at Albreda (*see pp64–5*), was representative of the fact that the whole area of Georgetown was free territory to anyone escaping French clutches.

Janjangbureh is surrounded by some exceptional freshwater riverine and savanna landscapes, and its biodiversity is attracting the attention of scientists and tourists alike.

Ruined colonial warehouses in Findlay Street, Janjangbureh

Kanilai

This small rural village has seen something of a renaissance in its fortunes in the last 15 years. It's the birthplace of President Jammeh, and his family still manages the large farm where he spent his childhood years. The family compound has developed into a kind of second seat for the president and his cabinet, and he often entertains foreign guests here.

For most of the year, visitors must be content with touring the **Kanilai Game Park**, which is currently in a state of serious disrepair. An eclectic mixture of African animals forms the basis of what, in the long term, will be a conservation programme for species under pressure elsewhere on the continent, though few are native to The Gambia. There are impala, wildebeest, ostriches and zebras, plus a breeding pair of rhinos. Less rare are the crocodiles, which congregate in large numbers around the freshwater pools. Access to the park is by vehicle only, accompanied by a ranger. Both ranger (and vehicle if you don't have one) can be hired from nearby Sindola Safari Lodge (*see p156*), a luxurious place to stay by upcountry standards.

Kanilai comes alive with Jola dancers and Gambian wrestlers during the International Roots Festival in June (*see p24*) and other traditional get-togethers. The tourist office can provide details of dates.

Kanilai Game Park. Open: daily 7–10am, 5–7pm. Admission charge.

An old wooden house in the centre of Janjangbureh

Kerr Batch Stones

Though not as famous as the much-visited Wassu Stone Circles (*see p91*), Kerr Batch Stones do get the occasional tourist group. The site is fenced and tickets are sold by members of a family that acts as custodians; however, during the rainy season the family grows crops around the stones, and if no visitors are expected they'll allow their cattle to graze the parched stems. A series of seven or eight circles comprising thigh- to chest-height thick circular stones, the Kerr Batch circles are not the most visually impressive, but they do have one rare feature – a 2m (6^1/$_2$ft)-high double menhir (standing stone) or lyre stone, which looks like a giant V-for-victory two-fingered salute. Archaeologists still

Janjangbureh and the mid-river region

A cow inspects the Kerr Batch Stones

have no clue as to why the ancients should have erected a double stone; suggestions are that two important people may have died within a short space of time and were commemorated together. However, this is another mystery that may never be solved.

The family's compound also has an interesting museum with many artefacts relating to the tribal practices of the rural area. Local beadwork, musical instruments and domestic tools make a real impact, because if you travel the dirt roads linking the rural villages you see the very same items in daily use. The landscape has some wonderful arable savanna dotted with tiny settlements complete with *bantaba* (*see p18*) and dozens of smiling children.
Signposted from Nyanga Bantang. Open: daily 9am–5pm. Admission charge.

Kiang West National Park
One of The Gambia's least-visited national parks, the animals and plants of Kiang West currently benefit from the dire condition of the main route south of the river, meaning most travellers forging upcountry tend to use the faster north route. It's a pity, because the park has some excellent tracts of pristine savanna and deciduous woodland, with healthy populations of all the country's major land mammals including bushbuck, duiker, noisy baboons, hyena, caracals and warthogs (known here as bush pigs). If you don't get the chance to see bush pigs in the flesh – they travel in large, noisy family groups – you'll be presented with signs of their recent activity all around the park as they root through the mud and earth in search of

roots and tubers, leaving behind metres of ploughed terrain.

The River Gambia forms the northern boundary of Kiang West, where, as with most riverine parks in The Gambia, mangrove rules. Many naturalists come to catch sight of the secretive sitatunga, an antelope that's made a home in the salt marshes and river shallows, and it's still possible to see the endangered manatee.

Kiang West has several escarpments from where it's possible to get overviews of watering holes or valley floors. Vehicular access is limited and exploration involves trekking on foot along several well-worn footpaths. The best vantage point is at Tubabkollon Point (*tubabkollon* means 'white man's well', so called because the Portuguese founded a small trading station here) on the river in the northeast corner. This is an area where many of the land and mangrove animals mix together; however, it's quite a trek from the main road. Many visitors make a base at Tendaba Camp (*see p90*) and take a boat or walk into Kiang West from there with an expert guide to point the way. It's a 15km (9-mile) round trip on foot, but setting off early and making a day of it offers some great animal- and bird-spotting opportunities.

Access off south road 125km (78 miles) east of Banjul. Open: daily 8am–6.30pm. Admission charge.

Janjangbureh and the mid-river region

You'll have a lot of the Kiang West National Park to yourself

River Gambia National Park

It is interesting that many of The Gambia's most successful and acclaimed 'eco-projects' have been brought to fruition by the willpower and sheer bloody-mindedness of a few maverick individuals. Think of Eddie Brewer at Abuko, and English and Williams at Makasutu, for example. The same is true of the River Gambia National Park, a protected tract of watercourse surrounding the Chimpanzee Rehabilitation Trust. This programme was started by the late Stella Marsden (daughter of Eddie Brewer) in 1969 in response to the number of captive animals confiscated during a purge on the ownership of these wild apes by authorities in The Gambia. The project founded three independent chimp communities on small, uninhabited, mid-river islands, free from the pressure of predators and other primate species. Currently over

A mahogany tree beside the River Gambia

70 animals form the study group, being regularly monitored by teams of visiting project workers. Other than that, there is little human contact.

THE STONE CIRCLES OF SENEGAMBIA

Little is known about the ancient peoples of The Gambia, but what is certain is that their most obvious legacy proves them to be capable of social organisation. Over 100 sets of megalithic stone circles and many hundreds of menhirs (standing stones) dot the landscape upcountry, spreading into Senegal to the north. Each one has been designed and erected with great care, but to what purpose remains unclear. Most don't make it onto the tourist maps but they fascinate archaeologists and anthropologists searching for clues about our African ancestors. So little is known about their origins that estimated dates for their erection range from 1500 BC to AD 700 – this is one of the great unsolved mysteries of our age. All the circles comprise at least ten stones.

They could herald the coming of the rainy season (very important in this part of Africa), simply mark the passage of time, or pinpoint the burial place of important tribal leaders; artefacts found during excavations include spear tips and precious metal, suggesting a sacred place or perhaps the place of interment of a high-ranking individual.

All the stones are hand-cut from deep brown igneous rock found all over this vast region, so they were not transported across vast distances. But they did have to be shaped and manoeuvred into place, which would have required a great deal of time and application.

Boat tours upriver lasting a couple of hours run from Janjangbureh (*see pp81–4*), and you may be lucky enough to spot chimps in the trees at the water's edge; or you can book a specialist stay at the Visitor Camp (*see p156*), where you can interact with the project workers and follow their work (though you cannot make footfall on the islands or meet the chimps themselves). You can also 'adopt' a chimp if you want to provide financial help to the project.

Interestingly, some of the last hippopotamus populations along the river have begun to find a home in the safe waters of the park. It's thought that up to 100 of these huge river dwellers are still found within Gambian territory, but they are spread along much of the upriver stretch and remain elusive.

280km (174 miles) upriver from Banjul. Chimpanzee Rehabilitation Project, www.chimprehab.com

A tour boat in River Gambia National Park

Soma

Farafenni's counterpart on the south side of the river, Soma isn't as large or as fast-paced as its northern rival, being little more than a couple of intersections flanked by cheap food stalls, truck-repair shacks and petrol stations. It's a good place to stock up on snacks for the continuation of your journey.

Tendaba Camp

Tendaba means 'big wharf' in Mandinka, and this simple jetty is one of the very few landing points along this stretch of the river. Set on the edge of Tendaba village is Tendaba Camp, a mecca for birdwatchers and naturalists who use it as a base for explorations of the parks on both the north (Bao Bolong – *see pp65–7*) and south (Kiang West – *see pp86–7*) banks in this region. The overnight accommodation is basic, but it's a place for like-minded people to sit together in the balmy evenings swapping notes and discussing tomorrow's programme. There's a restaurant and an atmospheric little bar by the water's edge. You can join a group on a set itinerary or hire a boat and explore at your own pace. There are more than a few knowledgeable guides at Tendaba who'll help you get the best out of exploring the wilds of The Gambia.
Tel: 991 1088. Open: daily.

Bush rooms at Tendaba Camp

The multifarious Wassu Stone Circles

Wassu Stone Circles

The finest set of ancient stone circles in West Africa, Wassu Stone Circles form the largest complex of monumental structures in The Gambia and are impressive not for their gargantuan size, but for their number and the overall beauty of the site. More than 100 stones make up a series of circles that range in size from 4–6m (13–20ft) across. The stones are slender and more graceful than those at Kerr Batch (*see pp85–6*), most standing above 1.5m (5ft). One circle outranks the others in size with a series of well-

carved monumental menhirs; however, it does not seem to sit in any position of authority within the site as a whole.

The compound has a small museum explaining how the circles were physically created. If you travel as part of a guided tour, you'll have a musical accompaniment to your trip as a couple of young *balafon* players give renditions of traditional tunes.

At Wassu you should leave a small stone atop one of the large standing stones to ensure good luck.
Wassu village. Open: daily 8am–6pm. Admission charge.

Boat tour: Upriver to Janjangbureh

The River Gambia is an extremely underutilised resource, both for transport and for tourism. It's the perfect conduit for exploration because nothing is very far from the water.

Unfortunately, not many boat tours are available, but one company, Jane's Boats (see p155), runs group trips at the end of the main tourist season and before the rains begin. The large double-decker pirogue can be your hotel and restaurant along the route; you'll sleep on deck under mosquito nets – how much closer to The Gambia could you be?

Allow 4–5 days.

Distance: 300km (186 miles).

1 Oysters
Your boat will depart from Denton Bridge along Oyster Bolong. As you turn left along Turnbull Bolong you will get your first view of the vast expanse of the lower reaches of the River Gambia.

Look out for the oyster harvesters who work in the mangrove roots where the oysters live, cutting them free with machetes. As you reach the river, you'll see Banjul city to the left.

The boat will then turn inland (east). As you pass Dog Island, look out for dolphins in this stretch of the river; they'll probably come to investigate the boat. After four or five hours' sailing you'll put in at Albreda.

2 Albreda
Here you can follow the Roots Trail. Learn about the slave trade and meet the Kinte clan – said to be the direct descendants of Kunta Kinte, ancestor of author Alex Haley (*see pp76–7*). As you leave Albreda look out for James Island, departure point for thousands of slaves shipped to the other side of the Atlantic. *Your boat continues pushing upriver and the banks will slowly begin to come closer together. It's a full day's sail to the next stop at Tendaba Camp.*

3 Tendaba Camp
Tendaba is a world-renowned birding centre (*see p90*) in close proximity to two exceptional protected areas, Kiang West and Bao Bolong. You can rent

a smaller boat and take a guide to spend the morning exploring the maze of narrow *bolongs*.
A few hours further east, if it's Sunday make a stop at the Yetilenda/ Bambatenda ferry jetty and take a taxi to Farafenni.

4 Farafenni

The country market or *lumo* held here (*see p81*) is one of the largest in the country and a fantastic cultural experience.

East of the ferry, the river begins to meander across a wide flood plain. Here the forest really begins to come into its own with lush mangrove and high stands of riverine forest. The birdsong is bright and varied, vying for air with the barking of baboons and other monkey calls, and there's little human activity.

Below the town of Kuntaur lies Baboon Island, a major eco-project.

5 River Gambia National Park

A collection of several mid-river islands makes up the River Gambia National Park (*see pp88–9*), which is home to the Chimpanzee Rehabilitation Trust. You'll not be allowed to land on the islands but you may spot chimps on the banks. The national park also protects a small population of hippos.
After the national park, the boat plies on, rounding a major bend at Kuntaur before the final turn to Janjangbureh.

6 Janjangbureh

As Georgetown this was Britain's eastern colonial outpost and a haven for freed slaves (*see pp81–4*). Now it's a sleepy town set among magnificent riverine ecosystems.

Boat tour: Upriver to Janjangbureh

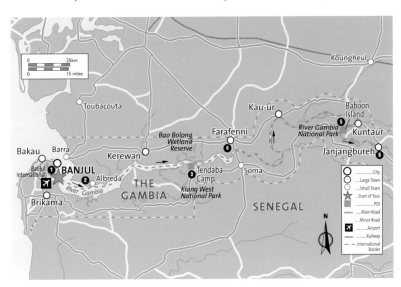

Walk: Janjangbureh

Georgetown once rivalled Bathurst in importance. It was Great Britain's upriver command post from the 1820s and was a vital administrative and trading settlement. Set on mid-river McCarthy Island, it became a haven for freed slaves after the British Empire abolished the practice.

Allow 1 hour. Distance: 1km (¹/₂ mile).

Start from the jetty of the vehicle ferry at the northeast end of the town.

1 Vehicle ferry jetty

Get to McCarthy Island aboard one of the characterful ferries that ply the River Gambia. Spending an hour or two people-watching at the ferry dock allows you to watch the ebb and flow of daily life upcountry.

Walk up the concrete jetty to where it meets the road. To the right stands the remains of the Maurel & Prom building.

The vehicle ferries can only take a couple of cars at a time

2 Maurel & Prom building

A large and dour warehouse built in the late 1800s (*see p83*), the Maurel & Prom building is not old enough to have had any connection with the slave trade. However, you may be approached by a 'guide' who will regale you with stories of cruelty and imprisonment.

Walk straight on past the building and after 50m (55yds) you'll reach an intersection. Just ahead, slightly to the left, is a small triangular garden with a young sapling at the centre. This is the Freedom Tree monument.

3 Freedom Tree

The legend of the monument says that any captive that broke free from his shackles and touched this tree could not be taken into slavery (*see p84*). Because Georgetown was surrounded by hostile enemy territory – that of the French who still worked the slave trade – the town literally ensured freedom for any African who could swim across to the island.

Continue on inland past the Gamtel office, then turn first right at a dust road.

4 Commissioner's Offices and Residence

On the left here is The Gambia's high-security prison, while on the right are the remains of the Commissioner's Offices and Residence. Once the most prestigious building in the town, the shell is now badly neglected.

Walk on down the lane, and after 170m (185yds) you'll reach the campus of Armitage School.

5 Armitage School

Inaugurated in 1927, the school catered to colonials and the Gambian elite; it still attracts boarders from around the country.

Retrace your steps back to the Maurel & Prom building. With your back to the building, walk down Findlay Street, which lies straight ahead.

6 CFAO buildings

The vast façades on the left overlooking the river belong to the CFAO buildings (*see p83*), a rival set of colonial warehouses to the Maurel & Prom. They're much more elegant in their form, though still only bare skeletons of buildings.

Continue down Findlay Street, and after another 150m (165 yds) the street turns sharp right.

7 Wesleyan Methodist Church

On the right here you'll see the simple form of the Wesleyan Methodist Church. This was the only outpost for this small Protestant denomination in Western Africa, and the Wesleyans were an important element in the early success of Georgetown.

At the end of the road here turn right on Owen Street to find yourself back at the Freedom Tree, then turn right to return to the ferry jetty.

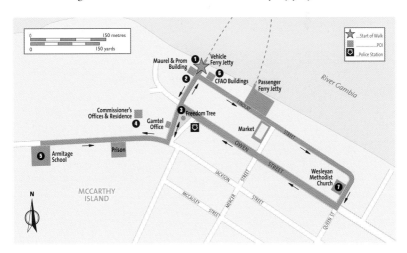

Organised tours in The Gambia

There are many possible tours you can take while in The Gambia, whether your interest lies in the natural environment, the wildlife or the everyday lives of the Gambian people.

Bolong tours

Creeks known as *bolongs*, bedecked with mangrove, form by far the most common natural ecosystem along the river, and you really haven't been to The Gambia unless you've spent some time on the water surveying the mass of tangled brown roots and verdant mantle. *Bolongs* are a vital resource for native birds and animals and hundreds of species of visiting birds. Under threat around the world, the mangrove ecosystems in The Gambia are becoming increasingly important on account of their pristine nature.

The tourist coast

In the Kombos you can join a group boat tour of the *bolongs* of the Tanbi Wetlands on a large double-decker pirogue. Early starts are best for birdwatching because, around dawn, there's a lot of activity as roosting birds wake. Of course, not everyone is interested in species counts and spotting a rarity, but it's surprising how

many people who've never thought about visiting a bird reserve get hooked when on one of these trips.

But birdwatching isn't the only reason to book a tour. Take an afternoon cruise for a spot of sunbathing on deck with the breezes cooling the air, or book a special sunset trip with cocktails and canapés to simply enjoy the views and the tranquillity.

Bolong trips from Makasutu Culture Forest (*see pp52–4*) take place in dugout pirogues, powered by small engines and seating around six to eight people, in which you sit very close to the water and get much more of a feel for your surroundings. As part of a day of activities, you'll enjoy a 30-minute outing on the water, but visit as an individual and you can negotiate a longer and more detailed tour.

You can rent kayaks from Denton Bridge Watersports (*see p149*) at Denton Bridge, to power yourself into the *bolongs* of Tanbi – though you'll have a guide so you don't get lost. These smaller craft allow you much closer access to the banks and narrow tributaries, and you can dictate your own pace. The centre also has wave runners, but do be aware that travelling at high speed on these craft will create waves that can disturb birds and other life on the shore margins. Use them as a vehicle for stealth rather than as an instrument of speed.

Upriver

Upcountry, *bolong* trips are a totally different affair. From Tendaba Camp (*see p157*), the *bolongs* of the national parks at Kiang West and Bao Bolong are within easy reach and the ecosystems are so much more varied than along the coast. Here the trips don't just take a couple of hours but can last up to a whole day, taking you to places little visited by humans. Only a small number of visitors to The Gambia make it upcountry, usually in small groups, so small craft and pirogues are the norm.

You also have the option of hiring a pirogue for a private visit where, once again, you have the advantage of dictating the pace and locations where you put ashore. This will give you maximum opportunity for, perhaps, sightings of hippos or clawless otters. Your guide will be able to take you to the most likely locations and you can spend as much time as you want once there.

Pirogues moored in Mandina Balong

Bush safaris

Not the grand journeys across open treeless plains in search of big game that you find in Kenya or South Africa, cross-country or bush safaris in The Gambia are much more low-key, but no less enjoyable. Take a cross-country trip from your coastal hotel, book a vehicle and driver to head upcountry or take to the trails on foot. There's a lot to see.

On the coast

Most tour operators on the coast run cross-country excursions in sturdy old army trucks with seating in the back,

which are ideally suited to the terrain. They traverse the dusty and potholed tracks with ease, while the high vantage point and open sides mean you get an excellent view of the passing villages and fields. Once off the main arterial route, the villages become remarkably rural very quickly, with family compounds clustered together and surrounded by small arable fields.

For a more sedate perambulation, take the camel safari from the base at Tanje village (*see p57*). These 'ships of the desert' take a route down the beach, in the shallows among the Atlantic flotsam and jetsam. It's quite a serene feeling once you get used to the movement; it's the getting up and down from ground level that can cause spills.

Upcountry

Although The Gambia is a small country, the landscape upcountry is big, with plains of giant baobab and silk cotton trees, a proliferation of deciduous forest, and tall grassland spreading out north and south of the river. Here, away from the major highways, there are no black-top roads.

Tour group in a truck

Baobab trees in the savanna

This is a fascinating area to explore, though it's wise to hire a 4WD vehicle and engage a guide if you don't want to spend hours lost along the way. Routes range across dried seasonal lakebeds or through grassland savanna, and the dust can be very debilitating during the dry season; the rainy season can see routes turn into a quagmire of clawing red mud which makes travelling much more difficult.

The national parks upcountry have limited vehicular access, but knowing these routes can make journeys on foot to find wildlife a lot shorter.

Trekking cross-country is really the only way to get to certain useful vantage points such as Tubabkollon Point (*see p87*) in Kiang West National Park, or the bird hide at Bao Bolong. Kiang West is easily reached overland from Tendaba Camp in two or three hours, and exploring a park at walking pace allows you to follow up every rustle in the undergrowth or tweet in the canopy. Make sure that you come with sturdy shoes, comfortable clothing and a hat. Don't forget a decent pair of binoculars, and take water and snacks because there is no provision at all in the parks.

Village visit

For anyone who wants to learn more about the culture and lifestyle of the peoples of The Gambia, there's nothing

Organised tours in The Gambia

more illuminating than a visit to a village. Though the building methods may vary from concrete in the west to mud and thatch in the east, most villages follow the same social system. Each village has several important locations that can also act as a social/meeting place. For men it is the *bantaba* – a large wooden or metal bed or couch usually placed under the ample shade of the largest silk cotton tree in the village. Here the men spend many hours discussing the issues of the day.

The village well is a focal point for the women. The Gambian authorities have worked hard to provide villages with modern hand-pump systems, which have made life easier. The women need to fill containers at least once every day, or take washing to be pummelled and pounded, and it's a

A village woman and her children cleaning rice

great opportunity to pass the time of day and have some fun.

The mosque is, of course, the spiritual centre of the community, with Friday lunchtime being when all the men of the village gather together to pray. Mosques are often very humble buildings, but perhaps the only one built of brick or concrete in the village.

If you visit the **Sifoe Kafo Farm**, a beekeeping cooperative at Sifoe near Brikama, you'll then go on to visit one of the family compounds of the women who work there – exactly which one is chosen by lots at the time of your visit, which is pretty egalitarian – and you'll be welcome to explore the family home. During the day the family, usually two or three wives with several children, live outside. A couple of *bantabas* serve as seating and food preparation areas. You'll be invited into the simple buildings that serve as bedrooms. Each wife has her own room, while the children sleep together. Behind the sleeping quarters are the animal shelters, one for the fowl and another for the goats and sheep.

You can be sure that wherever you decide to get out of your vehicle, you'll be surrounded by a group of young children shouting '*toubab*' and trying to take your hand as you stroll, asking quick-fire questions like 'What is your name?' and 'What is your country?' Most will want a little something – be it your plastic water bottle, a pen or some sweets. It's difficult to give to one without a flood of others assuming you have an unending supply of whatever you've given away. Still, you have to remember how little these children have and, especially upcountry, how exciting it is to be given even small items that are a rare commodity in the local community.

School visit

Schooling is not compulsory in The Gambia, though the government recommends that all children over the age of seven receive some kind of formal education. Many families are too poor to send their children to school, but with the country hoping to springboard into the 21st century it is imperative that this latest Gambian generation is able to take advantage of any opportunities presented by Jammeh's dreams for his country.

Without resources, many schools are poorly equipped to engender the necessary changes, and a visit to a local

Organised tours in The Gambia

Schoolchildren in Juffureh

school, either privately or with a tour group, brings home the great divide in educational provision between the developed and developing worlds. Books and materials are scarce and classrooms more so. Many early-stage classes have 100 pupils, while older children usually share lessons with 50 others. Pay for teachers is woefully inadequate when compared to ready-money jobs in the tourist industry, though there are many dedicated individuals trying to make a difference in the education system. The education of girls is seen as a primary concern. Girls are often kept at home while boys receive what little education a family can afford, but women are the primary carers for young children and are therefore important role models.

All the major tour operators have 'adopted' a local primary school to be included in their cultural tours, and you'll be allowed to visit the classrooms full of smiling pupils; they may even sing a welcome to you. Many people take materials such as books and pens (though pencils are better because work can be rubbed out and books used again, whereas ink leaves a permanent mark), and repeat visitors often come well prepared with old textbooks, maps and posters. The pupils learn in English, so anything designed for the UK National Curriculum, including resources produced by commercial companies, will be welcomed. Visitors without resources usually leave cash, but of course it's very difficult to monitor where the money goes once you leave the school compound.

The SOS Children's Village in Bakoteh is also featured in many tour

Children gather to sing for visitors

A typical bush schoolroom

itineraries. It's a marked contrast to the government-funded schools: well-dressed children in classrooms full of books, posters and smart new desks. There are even TVs with video players to enhance the learning experience. What has to be remembered is that most of the children here are without the traditional family support system that's so important in The Gambia, so they need the solid start in life that SOS can provide. Remember also that, because SOS is an international organisation, any donations you give will be accounted for in a professional manner.

Some visitors feel so moved by the obvious lack of educational opportunities in The Gambia that they form a very personal relationship with a given school, raising money and organising the delivery of regular supplies of paper, pens, pencils etc. But what is certain is that, no matter how often visitors are moved to help individual pupils or individual schools, education has to be one of President Jammeh's most pressing long-term issues.

The animals of The Gambia

Though the range of animal species found in The Gambia isn't as impressive as its tally of birds (*see pp58–9*), with only 108 cited mammal species, the possibility of easy viewing of several exotic creatures far outweighs the lack of variety.

You don't need to venture too far from the hotels of the Kombos to encounter endearing troops of monkeys. The Gambia has large numbers of vervets, colobus and red patas that frequent the grounds of the large hotels and wait for handouts of peanuts. Monkeys are easy to spot at Abuko, and close to the Senegambia Hotel is Bijilo Forest Park (*see p154*), where the inhabitants are pretty tame.

Larger and more belligerent are the baboons that range the countryside in troops. The infants and juveniles are as cute as the monkeys but the large dominant males can be aggressive and shouldn't be approached.

The shoreline and the river

Fiddler crabs are by far the most common shoreline creatures, sifting the mud banks for nutrients. In the water, look out for Atlantic humpback dolphins that roam the straits between Banjul and James Island.

Rarer species often only seen on tours into the national parks are clawless otters, hippos – which are now thought to be only around 100 in number – and manatees (sea cows), water mammals related to the elephant, now very rare but still inhabiting the mangrove shallows.

Inland

Upcountry you find the ubiquitous monkeys and baboons along with a healthy population of warthogs (a wild member of the pig family), which live in family groups called 'sounders'. Equally abundant are squirrels, and antelope species such as duikers.

Less numerous and not so easily seen are hyena and caracal (a lynx-like wild cat). One animal never seen by the casual visitor is the leopard. Although it is said to inhabit The Gambia, numbers are unknown and sightings are rare.

By night

At night, bats are king. Smaller species are the tourist's friend because they eat masses of mosquitoes, but the largest is the fruit bat, also known as the flying fox, which plays an important role in seed dispersal. Bushbabies inhabit the nocturnal world at Kiang West (*see pp86–7*), but you'll need a specialist guide to find them.

Reptiles

In addition to crocodiles, The Gambia has some fantastic reptile species; in excess of 74 have so far been documented. The monitor lizard can reach over 2m (6¹/₂ft) in length and is most easily spotted on the riverbanks or around waterholes. There are 41 species of snake, including spitting cobras, green mambas and carpet

FEEDING THE MONKEYS

The authorities in The Gambia are trying to dissuade visitors from offering food because in the long term it may cause monkeys to lose their fear of humans, and they may develop a dependency on the handouts rather than hunting for roots, fruit and nuts in the wild. It may be worthwhile discussing these issues with your children before they get caught up in a situation where they will just ache to offer a peanut or two.

vipers. The most common lizard is the agama, but you could also see geckos and chameleons.

The Gambia is a great place for spotting lizards

Getting away from it all

Tourism is highly developed in the far southwest corner of the country and there is a reasonably well-worn tourist trail east to Janjangbureh. East of McCarthy Island, however, you really are off the beaten track.

The far east of The Gambia

In this continental corner of The Gambia society is 100 per cent agrarian, with small villages scattered across the countryside, where women tend the fields while the men chew the fat on their shady *bantabas*. It couldn't feel further away from the bustle and push of the coast. This is a flavour of the true heart of Africa.

Bansang

An unremarkable settlement, but famed in birdwatching circles for the breeding population of red-throated bee-eaters that inhabit the walls of a nearby disused quarry.

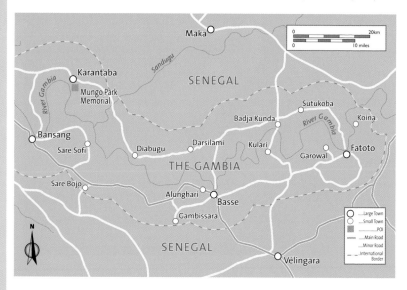

Wind down with a spot of fishing

The area also has healthy seasonal populations of carmine bee-eaters.

Basse

The 'capital' of the eastern region, Basse is where the tarmac road runs out. There are no actual attractions, but the vehicle ferry means it's a focal point for traffic and it's always busy. The town has been a centre of weaving and pottery for generations and you can watch the artisans at work and buy from roadside stalls. Birdwatchers visit Basse for its healthy numbers of Egyptian plovers.

Fatoto

The easternmost town of any size in The Gambia should be visited for its 'end of the world'-type atmosphere. There's a *lumo* (country market) every Sunday, but other than that it's a sleepy little place.

MUNGO PARK

Born in Selkirk, Scotland in 1771, Mungo Park qualified as a doctor but also developed an interest in botanical fieldwork. In 1788 he founded The Linnaean Society (now the leading society in the world for the study of taxonomy) with his friend Joseph Banks.

In 1794, Park heard that an expedition to discover the source of the River Niger had stalled because of the death of its leader. He offered his services and was accepted as a replacement. Park arrived in The Gambia in June 1795, and travelled 200km (124 miles) upriver to Pisania to recommence the project. On 21 July 1796 he reached the Niger at Segu, the first European to set eyes on the river. He charted the course for 300km (186 miles) before returning to Scotland at the end of 1797, when he wrote *Travels in the Interior of Africa*, a detailed narrative of his trip.

Park was invited by the British government to undertake a second expedition to find the mouth of the Niger and he departed for The Gambia at the end of January 1805, reaching the Niger in August. Park set off downstream but was attacked by hostile natives and drowned at the Bussa rapids when his boat became too fast on the rocks.

Karantaba

Karantaba is the nearest settlement to what was once Pisania, a British upcountry trading post. It was from here that Mungo Park set off with his expedition to find and map the River Niger (*see p107*). A simple obelisk on the riverbank outside the village acts as a memorial to the explorer, who lost his life on the river he charted. Karantaba hosts a *lumo* every Wednesday, when the normally somnolent streets come alive with activity.

Senegal

Senegal is not only The Gambia's closest neighbour; it surrounds Gambian territory on three sides.

Many of the ethnic groups of The Gambia also settled in Senegalese territory, giving the two countries many things in common – but the colonial history of Senegal is very different, being French territory until 1960. Today, Senegal is resolutely francophone, in contrast to The Gambia, which is anglophone.

Tour operators in The Gambia organise several trips into Senegal, either for the day or for a night or two. It's also easy to travel between the two countries independently, taking a bush taxi to the border and picking up another one on the Senegal side (some car rental companies don't allow rental cars to cross the border). Currently, the British Foreign Office issues advisories against travel to the Casamance province south of The Gambia, so all roads lead north across the river.

Even a short trip into Senegal highlights several stark contrasts between the two countries. The wonderful roads are the first, with smooth, rut-free asphalt linking all the main Senegalese settlements. Second is the temperature. The climate of northern Senegal is influenced much more by its proximity to the hot and arid Sahara, and as soon as you leave the cooling effect of the River Gambia the thermometer starts to rise. Third, and most obvious, is the language. Though the ethnic languages are common to both Senegal and The Gambia, the official language of Senegal is French, and English-speakers are few.

Bath time on Sipo island in the Saloum Delta National Park

Woven baskets for sale in Senegal

Dakar

The Senegalese capital Dakar can be reached from The Gambia after a full day on the road. A city of one-and-a-half million people, it's a cultural centre of West Africa and the focus of Islamic pilgrimage. Recently the city has also become a musical capital on account of *mbalax* rhythms that have taken the world by storm.

The Institut Fondamental d'Afrique Noire (IFAN) has one of the finest anthropological collections in Africa, with galleries of tribal masks, ritual objects and art from many African ethnic groups, plus one of the most complete archives in the continent, dating back to the early colonial era.

Gorée Island, just 3km (2 miles) outside the city, is Senegal's James Island (*see pp68–71*), the final departure point for the New World for thousands of imprisoned Africans transported by both the French and the British. The buildings here are well preserved, from dour slave quarters to elegant mansions, and they house several museums including the **Maison des Esclaves**, **Historical Museum**, **Fort d'Estrées** and **Musée de la Mer**.

In 2010, the **African Renaissance Monument** (*Route de l'Aeroport, Ouakam, Senegal; open: daily; admission charge*) was completed. It is a 49m (161ft)-tall bronze statue that stands just outside Dakar, overlooking the ocean. Built at a cost of £17 million, the imposing monolith has been heavily criticised by various Senegalese groups for its tremendous cost, dubious aesthetics, the fact that it was built in North Korea, and for its quasi-idolatrous rendering of a semi-nude man and woman. It is certainly worth seeing though!

For shopping, Kermel Market is a great place to browse for souvenirs and is famed throughout West Africa for its fabrics and good-value local clothing.

Saloum Delta National Park

The closest town to the Gambian border is Toubacouta, a tiny resort with a couple of hotels set in the heart of the Saloum Delta National Park, a biosphere reserve of 76,000ha (187,800 acres). Sandy islands and masses of mangrove on the seaward boundary give way to deciduous savanna inland. Pelicans and flamingos are among the major draws, but the park also has populations of 36 mammal species, including manatees and dolphins.

Saly

This seaside resort on the Senegalese coast south of Dakar has some wonderful beaches, top restaurants and a range of hotels. It is a popular holiday destination with numerous activities on offer including golf, surfing, fishing, horse riding, sailing, kayaking, jet-skiing and buggy tours. Nearby, about 16km (10 miles) to the east, is the **Bandia Nature Reserve**, a 1,000ha (2,471-acre) wildlife park that offers a fenced sanctuary for native animals including giraffes, rhinos, zebras, antelopes, impala and ostriches. You can take your own car into the reserve or hire the services of a guide and 4WD vehicle.

Bandia Nature Reserve. Off the main Dakar–Mbour road (N1).
Tel: (221) 685 5885. Open: daily sunrise–sunset. Admission charge.

View from Dakar across to Gorée Island

When to go

The Gambia has two main seasons – the rainy season and the dry season. The rhythm of life in the countryside is ruled by when the rains arrive and when they stop, and so, to a certain extent, is the tourist season. The climate of the coastal strip is influenced by the proximity of the ocean, while upcountry conditions are swayed by the pressure systems at work in the heart of the African continent.

The dry season

The dry season starts in October and runs into June on the coast, but ends perhaps a month later in the east. Note that, although daytime temperatures vary little between the rainy and dry seasons, the night-time temperatures drop quite dramatically in the dry season – enough for Europeans to need a light sweater while local Gambians pile on whatever warm clothing they have. As the name suggests, during the dry season there is very little rain and there is a subsequent drop in humidity and in mosquito numbers. As the dry season progresses the vegetation gets much sparser and drier, and the countryside takes on an almost sepia-tone hue, with parched leaves and dusty river beds.

The rainy season

From June to mid-October rainfall is much higher. It isn't like a constant monsoon but it falls in hard storms, filling up the city streets and creating inland lakes upcountry where rice crops are quickly planted. Between storms, the sun shines as brightly as ever, sucking up the water, so humidity rises rapidly with the rains, and nights become hot and sticky. The number of mosquitoes increases and dirt roads become boggy messes, but, on the upside, crops grow

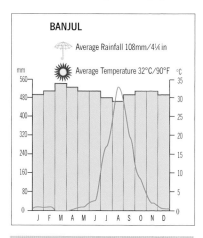

WEATHER CONVERSION CHART

25.4mm = 1 inch

$°F = 1.8 × °C + 32$

rapidly and the country is filled with beautiful wild flowers that in turn attract insects such as butterflies.

When to visit

Most charter flights to The Gambia run from the beginning of November until early May, coinciding with the lushest period of the dry season, when temperatures are pleasant to warm and humidity is low. These are the best conditions for building up a tan on the beach or spending days in the national parks, birdwatching or animal spotting.

Christmas and Easter are the busiest periods, while cut-price flights and

THE HARBINGER OF THE RAINS

The mighty baobab has long been the farmer's friend. Throughout the dry season it stands bare and skeleton-like, but it comes into leaf just before the rains start – so new foliage heralds the imminent end of the yearly drought.

packages are easiest to find for the first few weeks or last few weeks of the season.

Between late May and late October, the tourist infrastructure almost closes down, so accommodation is difficult to find and few restaurants and bars are open.

The beginning and end of the dry season are good times to visit – warm but not crowded

Getting around

Getting around The Gambia is quite a challenge. With no internal flights, trains or upriver ferries, you are pretty much limited to horsepower, literally or figuratively, to get you where you want to go. The infrastructure is painfully in need of investment, with dire road conditions and a lack of road signs and decent maps. Patience is needed as cross-country journey times can be long, but local transport along the tourist coast is cheap, plentiful and relatively reliable.

Local taxis

These bright yellow vehicles, also called 'bush taxis' or 'shared taxis', are the basic form of public transport for Gambians. They come in all shapes and sizes from rusty old Renault 4s to 'new to The Gambia' minibuses, all with a capacity of 'however many can squeeze into the seats'. Bush taxis run along set routes but pick up and drop off anywhere along this route. Passengers pay for the distance travelled plus for each item of baggage they carry, and fares are paid when you get off. Journeys are cheap and it's a great way to meet the locals.

If you don't rent a car or a car and driver, long-distance bush taxis are the only way to travel around upcountry, but even then they don't go regularly to every settlement. You'll need to plan your journey or be flexible about exactly when and where you travel. Taxis are often laden with crops, and even animals, as well as people;

tethered chickens along with goats and kids are regular baggage. For long-distance journeys you'll pay before you travel, and fares and baggage fees are open to negotiation. If there are many taxis on the same route you'll be accosted by touts trying to get you into their vehicles, but be aware that bush taxis don't leave until full, so you may have a long wait if business is slow.

It may be quicker to hire the whole taxi to yourself – private hire – rather than wait until the taxi is full and have passengers being dropped off and picked up along your route. To find an empty taxi, you'll need to go to the taxi garage – normally near the market in towns – to negotiate a price.

One thing is for sure: there are reliability issues with bush taxis and you'll often see one or more broken down at the roadside with passengers waiting patiently for help to arrive. Breakdowns are just something else to factor into a road trip and seem to be accepted by Gambians themselves.

Tourist taxis

Bush taxis aren't allowed to enter some sections of the tourist coast, notably the Senegambia Strip and Cape Point. A specially licensed fleet of green-coloured vehicles services the hotels. Tourist taxis are supposed to be more reliable, newer vehicles, and drivers have to prove they have insurance. The drivers also speak good English and can help with planning itineraries. Tourist taxis are more expensive than bush taxis (at least three times the price and sometimes ten times as much), but they offer return-journey prices with a certain amount of waiting time included, so you can allow time for a visit to an attraction or a meal out in

TAXI ETIQUETTE

If trying to flag down a taxi, don't stick out your thumb as you would if you were trying to hitch a lift; this action is considered rude in The Gambia. Hold your hand out and wave it up and down. If the driver has capacity he'll stop for you, and if not he'll speed on by.

the evenings. Prices are posted at the rank outside every hotel so there's no need for negotiation; however, if you want to engage a driver for the day, it pays to barter over the price.

Ferries

With just four crossing points – only one of which is a bridge (*see p83*) – the River Gambia presents an enormous barrier to travel, not just for Gambians but also for the Senegalese who must cross Gambian territory to reach their

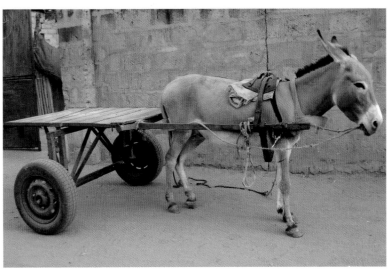

Many Gambians still rely on literal horse – or donkey – power

southern provinces. The two vehicle ferries crossing from Banjul to Barra are the largest in the country, but cars still have to wait at least four hours to cross, and commercial traffic up to a week. The Yelitenda/Bambatenda ferry is the second major crossing point, with a preponderance of Senegalese truck traffic, while the two tiny ferries to Janjangbureh (which can also be reached from the south by a bridge) take no more than two to four cars each at any one time.

Currently, there are no ferries carrying passengers up and down the river.

Car rental

Car rental is not widespread in The Gambia, though it is possible to have one delivered to the hotel or pick one up at the airport. The lack of street signage and good maps makes navigation almost impossible in the Kombos, and the condition of the roads and tracks upcountry isn't for the faint-hearted or inexperienced.

Hiring a car and driver by the day or longer is much more common – though if you are travelling upcountry, clarify who will be responsible for driver meals and accommodation before you start the trip.

Ferry, Banjul port

A local bus laden with produce

A third option is to rent a taxi by the day. This works out better financially if you don't intend to undertake excursions every day: you are then paying for a vehicle only when you actually use it.

When choosing a vehicle, think about the journey you are going to undertake. For many routes 4WD makes sense, and for upcountry journeys something with 4WD and good suspension is imperative.

If you do decide to drive yourself, you should drive on the right and overtake on the left where possible, but be aware that, especially upcountry, drivers stick to the best possible road surface on any given stretch. Don't build up great speed on smooth sections as they don't last long and sudden, hard breaking can be dangerous. Keep a watchful eye out for other road users, and be careful of animals on the roads and potholes in the surfaces. After dark there is almost no street lighting anywhere in the country, so extra care is needed.

Travellers with disabilities

There are no specialised transport services for travellers with disabilities. Consult a ground operator such as Gambia Tours (*see p149*), who can help with the logistics.

Accommodation

The opening of the new Sheraton Gambia Resort Hotel & Spa at Brufut Beach in early 2007 set a new benchmark for accommodation in The Gambia, spearheading its repositioning in the tourism marketplace. Luxurious, true five-star hotels have since sprung up along the tourist coast south of the River Gambia's mouth.

The Gambia's tourist coast has a selection of accommodation in most price ranges. The earliest hotels do look a little dated with their block styling, but more recent builds have taken the setting into account and are much more sympathetic to the landscape. There are no high-rise monstrosities blighting the beaches, but lovers of 1970s architecture will feel right at home. Most hotels are enhanced by verdant gardens, and there are choices in all price ranges that have direct access to the beach.

Hotels in The Gambia use the international star rating system for quality, but be aware that ratings don't always match quality ratings in Europe or North America and should be used for comparison with other hotels in the country rather than with hotels abroad. Rooms are generally spotlessly clean in all categories, though at lower star ratings fittings may be careworn. Since the offshore undercurrents make swimming in the sea difficult, you may want to pay particular attention to pool size, especially if you have children.

All-inclusive packages (flight, room, meals and/or drinks) are an important part of holiday provision in The Gambia. This can represent value for money, but there is a good choice of eateries in the tourist areas for those who would rather choose a bed and breakfast rate.

In the last decade, the seeds of a new generation of upmarket eco boutique hotels have been sited here. These chic lodges make the most of their exotic location yet provide touches of luxury and personal service not seen before in the country, including room service and excellent food. They make fantastic romantic getaways and offer the chance of some quality 'me' time away from the crowds.

Upcountry, in the east of The Gambia, accommodation is limited to a few unpretentious lodges. You'll sleep in concrete or mud-brick round huts such as those at **Janjangbureh Camp**, or in strong canvas tents at **Bird Safari Camp** (*see p156*), which offer a bed, simple private facilities with toilet, sink and shower, and an evening meal. Some have plunge pools, but most simply represent somewhere to rest your head after a long day wildlife watching or travelling.

There is one campsite in The Gambia. **Sukuta Camping** (*see p149*) offers simple accommodation such as you find at the upcountry camps, but also has space for tents and motorhomes. It caters to the steady stream of intrepid travellers crossing the Sahara.

In all price categories, rack rates (walk-in rates) are high. The cheapest option, unless you can get a very cheap flight, is to book flight and accommodation together as part of a package with a major tour operator. One- and two-week packages represent excellent value for money and are discounted if there is late availability.

The Ocean Bay resort in Bakau

Food and drink

The mountains of fresh produce for sale in all the local markets are evidence of a robust local cuisine with some delicious dishes to try, but The Gambia doesn't have a book of set recipes. The staple dishes vary in the balance of ingredients depending on the season and the economic status of the family, but they are worth exploring.

Chillies for sale in Albert Market, Banjul

Gambian dishes

The basis of all Gambian cuisine is to take a good serving of a filling carbohydrate mixed with or topped by a small amount of a rich sauce containing meat or fish. The main carbohydrate is usually rice, but couscous (tiny pieces of durum wheat) or cassava are also common. Popular sauces include *domoda* (a rich peanut sauce) or *plasas* (a palm oil and cassava leaf or okra sauce). *Benachin* means 'one pot' in Wolof and is a dry rice risotto-style dish with varying amounts of meat or fish and vegetables. Jolof rice is similar but cooked with tomatoes and vegetables. Chicken *yassa* is available just about everywhere: the chicken is marinated in an aromatic mixture of chilli, garlic and lime to create a strong and zesty flavour.

Meat

Chickens, goats and sheep roam free even in built-up areas such as Serrekunda, and families will eat these

A restaurant in Kololi

on feast days and during celebrations. Meat on sale in butchers is *halal* (killed in accordance with Islamic law). It's usually lamb or beef and it's fresh each day. The Christian community is the only one to keep pigs, and they usually only service their own domestic needs.

Most meat served in hotels in the Kombos is imported because the country can't supply it on a large enough scale to meet the needs of the tourist industry.

Fish

Fish is always a good choice because the catches are landed every day. Bonga fish is most popular with Gambians because it is cheap and plentiful, but it has lots of small bones so isn't to everybody's taste. More commonly on restaurant menus you'll find butterfish and ladyfish – larger, more muscular fish with a firm texture. Bigger fish such as tarpon are also available, and prawns are farmed around Albreda. Try the *bolong* oyster in a soup or stew.

TIPPING

Waiters will certainly appreciate a tip. Leave the small change at bars and around 25 dalasi at dinner unless you are at a top restaurant, where a little more is the norm.

The local tipple from JulBrew

Drinks

Though most Gambians don't drink alcohol, The Gambia has its own domestic brewery, JulBrew, which opened in 1977 and makes very drinkable lager. The brewery also makes Guinness® under licence.

Kim Kombo distillery supplies small quantities of delicious tropical liqueurs that are unlike anything else on the market.

Tea is the drink of choice in most Gambian homes, and the ritual of making it is a time-honoured one (*see p18*). Sorrel flower petals are also infused to make a hot or cold drink (known as *wonjo*). Coffee is always Nescafé, served hot and strong.

Where to eat

Around the tourist coast there are hundreds of restaurants to choose from and they usually combine some Gambian cuisine with international dishes on their menus.

Once upcountry, international-style restaurants are almost impossible to find, but the main commercial districts will always have one or two basic eateries serving reliable staple Gambian dishes. The bush camps all serve food, generally a buffet with the main dish being a Gambian one.

Snacks are easier to find. At major intersections and around markets you can buy bags of cashews or peanuts, juicy peeled oranges, steamed cassava stalks, or fried dough balls with hot chilli sauce.

Vegetarians

Vegetarians are rarely specifically catered for in The Gambia but can usually still find something to suit. Pasta dishes with meat-free sauces are usually included on the menus in restaurants along the tourist coast, but often even dishes that one would assume are free from animal products, such as vegetable soups, are made with meat stock, so ask before you order.

Entertainment

The ethnic groups of The Gambia each have their own traditional tribal songs and dances that still perform an important function in modern life. Songs and dances relate to important rites of passage through life and turning points in the seasons. These thriving art forms offer visitors a rich vein of folkloric performances to enjoy.

The best place to see these songs and dances being performed is in situ in the villages upcountry during celebrations and rituals, but cultural or folkloric evenings in the resorts do a reasonable job of bringing the flavour and energy to a tourist audience. Try to visit the evening performance at Makasutu Culture Forest if you can, because the atmosphere and the setting make this the most magical of all the commercial shows.

Traditional village dance display

Musicians playing the *kora* and *balafon*

Music

In Mandinka society, the rights of story-telling and song are the sole domain of the *jeli* or *griot*, the traditional holder of the oral history. A *jeli* is called upon to perform at naming ceremonies, circumcisions and weddings as they have been for generations. They sing lilting songs illustrating the long history of the tribe and the family. Vocals are accompanied by the *kora*, a lute-type instrument made from a hollowed-out calabash with over 20 strings that is played with the strings facing the player. The repetition of simple refrains on the *kora* creates an almost Zen-like background sound and it is used in many hotels and attractions as an aid to relaxation.

Another very relaxing sound is that of the *balafon*, a xylophone-style instrument with wooden blocks of various sizes tied together between two stands that are tapped with wooden sticks to produce the sound. The deep resonance of the notes forms a base percussion canvas upon which the contrasting timbre of the *kora* and *riti* (*see below*) can paint a picture in sound.

The percussion is further beefed up by drums. Mandinka drums are traditionally three in number, of varying sizes from large to small; the big Wolof drums really pack a punch. It's a sound that fills the air and requires a lot of effort from the players themselves. The rather macho nature of drumming means that it's a popular pastime for young male Gambians, and you are bound to hear drum sounds booming through the air at least once every day during your visit. The most common drum played today is the *djembé*, which is made of a piece of wood hollowed out and shaped like an hourglass, with a taut goat skin stretched over one end, tied in place with cord. This skin is then tapped with the hand to produce the beat.

The Jola *riti* is a stringed instrument played with a bow like a violin, though the number of strings can vary from one to four. It produces a range of high-pitched sounds that accent the voices or the bass notes of the drums and *balafon*. Similar instruments are the *kotingo* and the *bolom*.

Different types of flutes made from wood, bamboo, calabash or clay also add a high note – these may be substituted for a whistle in modern music displays.

An instrument that is making a comeback is the *akonting*, another stringed, lute-like instrument made from a dried calabash that was the forerunner of the Western guitar. The **Akonting Center for Senegambian Folk Music** at Madinari village is a centre of excellence for this and other traditional Gambian music.

Mbalax music

One of the most popular and well-known genres of the modern 'world music' scene is the West African *mbalax*, which radiates out of Senegal but has several Gambian virtuosi. Here the *sabar* (Wolof tall drums) and *tama* (drum held under the arm) form the percussion soundtrack to the lilting reedy vocals of the *jelis* and the sound of the *kora*, but traditional West African sounds have been mixed with influences from the Caribbean such as reggae and ska. Youssou N'Dour is the most internationally famous *mbalax* musician, but there are many more to enjoy.

As *mbalax* itself has developed it has branched out into '*mbalax* rap' and '*mbalax* hip-hop', creating whole new musical tie-ups and yet more West African home-grown popular music.

Head to one of the market stalls selling CDs and tapes and ask them for *mbalax* music. You should be able to pick up sample albums for around £1 each.

Gambian dance

Most of the traditional Mandinka *griot* tales are for listening to, not for dancing to, but when it comes to the thundering beat of the drum solos, the dancers have something that fits the bill exactly.

A line or circle of clapping women builds the tension until one of them jumps into the sand lifting knees and elbows high in quick succession in rhythm with the drum strikes, pounding the ground with the heel on the down stroke. It's a high-energy movement that tires even the fittest dancer after 30 seconds or so, so as one dancer finishes, another steps into the arena to keep up the momentum. At its best the movement is so fluid that all you see is a puff of dust rising as the feet stomp down, and all else is just a blur of movement.

A fire-eating performance at Kololi Beach

A *kankurang* or spirit guide

In Jola tradition male dancers also perform very physical movements, such as back spins and head spins, that have influenced the modern body popping, body patting and hip-hop moves.

Many cultural performances also include the appearance of traditional spirit guides like the *kankurang* with his coconut matting costume, and the *kumpo* with his outfit of long rhun palm fronds with a pole pointing out of the top – both of which are said to protect against the effects and presence of evil in traditional communities. Stilted dancers and fire-eaters also add a touch of the dramatic.

Bars, clubs and discos

There is a good range of nightlife on the tourist coast with Irish-style pubs, karaoke bars and clubs for dancing, and these are open throughout the season. At the latest hotspots, the crowd is swelled at weekends by young urban Gambians. Local clubs featuring recorded or live *mbalax* are always busy at weekends and are a great way to get into the West African beat.

The nights start late here and most nightclubs don't open before midnight; however, there'll be no shortage of places to enjoy a couple of drinks before that, if you want to start a little earlier.

Shopping

For lovers of local handicrafts, The Gambia is a shoppers' delight, offering an exceptional range of artisan-produced items for every budget. You are bound to find something to suit your taste. The best items are both practical and beautiful.

Basketware

Grasses have traditionally been used to create natural containers in a range of sizes and colours. Choose anything from bread baskets to linen baskets.

Batik and cloth

Batik fabric is another traditional Gambian handicraft (*see pp130–31*) and you can buy it as art or made into clothing. Hand-woven cotton cloth in traditional tribal patterns is fashioned into table runners, place mats or shoulder bags.

Beads and bangles

The colourful barter beads that the colonial Europeans traded for slaves in the 16th and 17th centuries kick-started a fashion for beadwork in Africa that continues into the modern age. Original beads are now expensive and very hard to find, though some traders will assure you that they have the genuine article. More common are inexpensive strings worn as chokers, bangles or anklets.

Fetish items or *jujus*

The treatments prescribed by animist tribal witch doctors to increase spiritual strength and fight evil spirits, such as metal bangles and tooth and hair objects, have become such valuable collectibles that originals are difficult to find. Still, tourist stalls will normally

BARTERING

Bartering or bargaining is a fact of life in The Gambia. It isn't something that comes naturally to a shopper who is used to fixed prices, so here are some tips to make the bartering process more successful and enjoyable.

- To start with, look at several items and act cool about the specific item you want.
- Your first offer should be around 20 per cent of what the shop owner asks, then increase your offer little by little. You'll probably end up paying around 50–60 per cent of the original asking price.
- Keep smiling! This isn't a contest; it's a way of reaching agreement.
- If you don't want to pay the price, simply tell the shop owner and walk away.
- Once you agree a price it is very bad manners to change your mind!

sell newer versions featuring cowrie shells, bone and metal.

Music and musical instruments

Small souvenir *djembé* drums are sold at just about every tourist market stall, but you'll also find good-quality hand-made full-size drums, *balafon* (wooden xylophones) and exquisite *kora* (stringed lutes) on sale. Tapes and CDs of Senegambian *mbalax* music make an excellent addition to your collection.

Woodcarving

Woodcarving is a tradition passed from father to son and it's The Gambia's most popular handicraft. The quality of the work is very high, so it's simply a matter of finding something you like – from traditional tribal masks to crocodiles, elephants or decorative bowls. Traditional hardwoods such as mahogany or ebony are now almost impossible to find, so be aware that most dark woodcarvings are dyed with shoe polish.

Where to buy

The Gambia's craft markets or *bengdulas* are the place to find a full range of souvenirs and compare price and quality. You'll find a *bengdula* at every tourist resort, or at Serrekunda market or Albert Market in Banjul. Beach stalls and hotel souvenir shops also have a good choice of objects.

Bracelets for sale at Tanje Village Museum

Batik

Batik is the art of decorating cloth (usually natural cottons and silks) using wax and dye. It is practised in many countries around the world, each with their own ethnic patterns and images. The word batik originates from Java in Indonesia, where *tik* means 'to dot', and the technique in this Far Eastern country is to put the wax on the material by way of numerous taps of a pointed quill. The Portuguese were the first Europeans to see this technique outside Indonesia and simply imported the Javanese word to describe it. The technique in The Gambia is to use the quill to isolate large blocks of cloth, like a child colouring with crayons.

A batik artist at work

Traditional African ethnic patterns feature shapes and colours rather than 'pictures', but most batik found in the tourist markets along the coast features quite literal landscapes featuring rustic thatch huts, maidens carrying loads on their heads, or bright beach scenes with swaying palms.

The raw materials

The Gambia always had natural beeswax in abundance and mangrove leaves were used as a mordant. The earth gave up a palette of natural dyes in the beige and brown ranges, plus a strong indigo blue much in demand in Europe, which helped to create 'serge de Nîmes' or 'denim' (now synonymous with fashionable blue jeans). Today artificial paraffin wax is used more commonly in commercial operations because it's much more user-friendly. It melts at low temperatures and provides a longer working time before it solidifies. Artificial dyes may also be used, along with a chemical mordant, because they provide reliable colour relatively inexpensively.

Lost wax technique

First the pattern needs to be planned on the fabric. Any whites to be found

A finished piece of batik work

in the final finished piece are covered in wax by use of the metal 'quill', then the cloth is dipped in the first dye colour. Any element of the pattern to be kept the first colour is then covered in wax and the whole is dipped in a second, differently coloured, dye bath. To preserve elements of this second colour other sections are covered in wax before a third colour is added, and the process continues and the colour range expanded to produce ever more elaborate designs. When the pattern is finalised, the whole canvas is washed in boiling water, which seals the dye and melts the wax. The whole process is ecologically sound because the wax can be reused numerous times.

Tie 'n' dye or 'tie dye'

A traditional technique throughout much of Africa and Asia, 'tie dye' puts pattern onto fabric by a process of resist dying.

Resist dying uses some kind of barrier between cloth and dye so that parts take the colour and parts don't. In the case of tie dye, the fabric is bundled together and parts are tied with a strong rope, or the fabric is knotted, before it is immersed in the dye. The fabric at the heart of the knot or rope bundle resists the colour most, while a round wheel of colour, running light to dark, is created as a final pattern. Subsequent processes complicate and deepen the pattern and the colour.

Sport and leisure

Organised sport and leisure activities are not well developed in The Gambia, since relatively few Gambians can afford to spend money on hobbies and pastimes. However, the tourist development along the coast has stimulated provision of a range of activities catering specifically for visitors and these are expanding all the time as the industry develops and matures.

SPECTATOR SPORTS
Football (soccer)

Football is a major passion with Gambians. Television coverage of all the major leagues in Europe is available at local bars and sports clubs, for only a few dalasis a game, so you'll find favourite teams ranging from Arsenal to AC Milan and Barcelona to Bolton Wanderers. Almost every male Gambian between the ages of 6 and 25 wears a jersey with a player's name on the back – the modern uniform of youth – though royalties definitely aren't going back to the players and clubs for these endorsements.

Gambians are always happy to chat for hours about football and there are several minor amateur leagues for players, but the professional game isn't very well developed, so there's little chance of seeing a good live game. The best matches are held at the Independence Stadium in Bakau on Saturdays in the dry season. The national team is currently managed by Belgian Paul Put but it makes no impression, even in the pan-continental African Nations Cup competition, when compared to the likes of Nigeria and Cameroon.

Independence Stadium

The huge **Independence Stadium** in Bakau is a rather grand venue for all manner of sports and social events, including football cup finals and a few international matches. It also hosts the finales of parades and political rallies.

Wrestling

Senegambian wrestling, or *borreh*, is classed as the national sport. Until President Jammeh came to power it was a dying art, but he has raised the profile and features it in most of the national festivals and events, so a few more young people are taking it up. It's not a sport that can be found on every street corner, however. The best time to see competitions is during

Local boys playing football in Tanje

diplomatic events held by the President at Kanilai.

The style is similar to that of Graeco-Roman wrestling, in which the combatants must try to throw their opponents through holds of the upper body only, rather than attacking the legs and lower torso. The contests can be ferocious and bloody, but, typically of any Gambian public spectacle, they have a theatrical backdrop with lots of drumming and tribal singing.

PARTICIPATORY ACTIVITIES
Birdwatching

By far the most popular leisure pastime for visitors, beyond lazing around on the beach, birdwatching is one of The Gambia's main tourist money earners.

The country has several advantages over its neighbours in that it has a range of ecosystems that attract birds, and a collection of protected areas where their habitat is not under threat. Government-licensed guides are helpful and knowledgeable and you can hire them by the hour or by the day. Guides can supply binoculars but it's far better to bring your own if you have them. Specialist birdwatching trips are easy to organise either before you depart for The Gambia or during your stay, through a ground tour operator such as Gambia Tours (*see p149*).

Cycling

Cycling is one of the most pleasurable ways to explore the countryside of

Bicycle rental in Kotu

The Gambia. On the tourist coast, attractions are not great distances from one another and the landscape is flat. Once off the major roads there's very little traffic and you can travel at your own pace.

There are cycle rental kiosks in all the major resorts and you can rent by the day or longer. Not all bikes are in the best possible condition, so check brakes and tyres before you set off. Cycle helmets are not generally available, so if you have one at home, bring it with you.

Cycling is also a good method of touring upcountry if you have the stamina. The southern arterial road inland is in such dire condition that cycling is probably the quickest form of transport, because you can steer around the potholes. This makes a great adventure if you are willing to stay in local villages on your travels.

Golf

There are two golf courses in the tourist area, though playing here is a little different to a round at home. Gambian course managers have long since given up on trying to irrigate vast tracts of countryside when water for crops can be in short supply, so 'greens' are 'browns' – and putting areas are kept impeccably by 'browns keepers' who rake and flatten them after every player has passed. Golfers 'drive' balls off rubber mats instead of teeing off from grass.

The **Fajara Club** (*see p47*) is a long-standing expat meeting place that, in addition to a par 69 18-hole course, also has tennis courts, squash and badminton facilities. It welcomes visitors (though you have to pay a temporary membership fee), who mostly come for the golf.

The **Kololi Beach Club** also has a par 54 18-hole course. It's a part-ownership holiday complex that opens to day visitors.

Horse riding

You can rent horses at Kotu beach for sunset treks along the strand. The riding is not difficult so it's suitable for all abilities, but it's not particularly challenging if you are an experienced rider.

Sport fishing

The rich, cool Atlantic waters offshore from The Gambia attract large numbers of fish – as witnessed by the catches landed by the fishing fleets every day. Sport fishing targets the largest of these species including barracuda, stingray, threadfin salmon (known locally as 'captain fish') and huge grouper, and anglers can spend a day pitting their wits and strength against these denizens of the deep. Onshore angling can be just as much fun, with companies providing equipment and guides so that you can find just the right site for a decent catch. The tidal mangroves make a challenging environment with their constantly changing water levels, and you can even fish directly off the beaches.

In the rough at Fajara Golf Club

Children

The Gambia makes a great destination for children. It offers a taste of life on the African continent combined with a beach holiday. There are fascinating landscapes and lifestyles to explore, and the warm sunny weather is a constant accompaniment to the daytime activities.

There are very few attractions specifically designed for children in The Gambia. Most young Gambians have few toys and no disposable income of their own. Even a simple football is a much sought-after item, possession of which is something most Gambian children can only dream about. Despite a lack of resources, Gambian children have a natural effervescence that's infectious. Upcountry, children from several family compounds usually play together. The environment is totally secure as there is always an adult around to keep an eye on the activity. Rolling metal bike hubs is a popular pastime, but most of the time children play make-believe or chase games.

Beach fun

The beaches along the tourist coast are soft and fine, so they are perfect for young children who just want to dig or make sandcastles. However, the seas have undercurrents, so, although paddling in the shallows is okay, keep swimming for the hotel pool. All the beaches around the major hotels have lifeguards on duty during the day, and there is a flag system where the red flag means that sea conditions are not suitable for swimming.

Animal encounters

Animal encounters are among the most enjoyable things about a trip to The Gambia. A visit to Abuko Nature Reserve (*see pp43–5*) or the monkey park close to the Senegambia Hotel is certain to result in sightings, and many animals are quite tame, although you should not feed them. Most hotel grounds have a few monkey inhabitants that are accustomed to visitors, and children just love it.

Older children with an interest in the natural world have a whole host of other fascinating creatures to enjoy. Rock agama lizards scoot and scurry along walls and into undergrowth, praying mantises lie motionless on branches, and birds are fun to watch.

Join in with the tribal drumming

The only problem is that children may have more questions than you can answer – there could be a budding naturalist in the family.

The Gambian upcountry national parks are less interesting for small children because of the sheer difficulty in getting to the sites and the amount of walking it takes to find the wildlife. It's possible to see hippos on boat trips upcountry but it's not guaranteed, so children need to have a lot of patience to wait for rewards that may not come.

The **Gambian Reptiles Farm** (*see p155*), located between the fishing villages of Gunjur and Kartong, has many different species of snake, lizard, crocodile and turtle. You may even get the chance to have a very close

encounter with a relatively harmless African royal python. For crocodiles, the sacred pool at Katchikally (*see p49*) is a must – this is definitely the closest your children should ever get to a live, fully-grown croc.

Folklore performances
The booming of the drums and the colourful costumes of traditional dances will captivate children. The beat is infectious and they're often among the first to volunteer to have a go if invited.

Jeep safaris
Children will love travelling around on the old army trucks and getting off-road with all its bumps and bounces. The high vantage point is excellent for

Children are always happy splashing about in the pool

children more used to standing well below adult eye level, and they can get a great view of everything that's happening as you travel along. All these trucks have seat belts, so it's wise to make sure that your children are well strapped in when the truck is on the move.

Funfair

There's a small funfair called **Dream Park** on Bertil Harding Highway, where it meets the Senegambia Strip. The park has a range of sit-on rides suitable for under-tens, and a visit here would certainly keep children happy for an hour or two.

Want a pen pal?

Gambian children will definitely want to get to know all about their contemporaries from other parts of the world, and your children might not be used to all the attention. Most Gambian

children want someone to write to – to practise their English – and if your children are in the market for a pen pal, it's a great place to find one. The children will have their address (usually a post box in Banjul where post for an extended family arrives, or sometimes a business address where one of the family works) printed on a scrap of paper. This could be one worthwhile and enduring souvenir of the trip.

Practicalities

The tourist hotels are geared up for families and will have high chairs in the restaurant. Restaurants along the coastal strip welcome children, but facilities such as high chairs are rare and child-specific menus are not that common.

One practical problem that parents will find is in pushing buggies around. Pavements are rare and those that exist are rutted and have high kerbs.

Roadside verges can be uneven and dusty, making progress slow and uncomfortable for child and parent.

Child health

You'll need to take a little extra care with children's health when you visit The Gambia, but there's no need to worry unduly. Speak to your doctor about malaria prophylaxis appropriate for the age of your children, and guard against mosquito bites during your trip. Make sure they wear insect repellent as the sun sets and after dark, and also if you venture into any of the nature parks or reserves.

Never underestimate the strength of the sun. Keep a high-factor cream on skin and reapply it after swimming. Make sure your child always wears a hat and protects his or her eyes with sunglasses.

Clean and cover any small cuts to prevent infection, and monitor any insect bites. If a young child develops diarrhoea make sure they drink plenty of liquids and call a doctor. Dehydration is a concern in any hot climate, so make sure your child is drinking regularly.

Children

Finding a pen pal isn't difficult!

Essentials

Arriving

All international flights, both charter and scheduled, arrive at Banjul International Airport, 15km (9 miles) south of the capital by road.

You will need to fill in an arrivals form. This may be given to you on the flight; it will be stamped and kept by the passport official. Most airline ticket prices now include a $10 entry tax (all UK charter companies now include it). If not, you'll need to pay it on arrival to the passport control official.

At the bag collection carousel you'll be pressured by the luggage porters. They charge a fixed £1 or $1 for their services but this includes putting your bags through the arrival X-ray machines and clearing them through customs, so it is worth using one to avoid the scrum. Tourist taxis are found outside the terminal building and these operate on a fixed fee basis.

Scheduled carriers to The Gambia include Brussels Airlines and Air Senegal International, but prices are incredibly expensive and not generally available on the main travel websites. Much more regular and much cheaper are the charter flights provided by the main package holiday companies including Thomas Cook (*www.thomas cook.com*) and Monarch (*www.monarch. co.uk*). The Gambia Experience (*www. gambia.co.uk*) is a company with a long relationship with the country, who fly there throughout the year – though flights aren't as frequent between May and October.

Departing

As of November 2010 there is a departure tax of €20 or equivalent levied when you leave The Gambia. At the time of writing this is not included in ticket prices and must be paid at the airport.

Passports and visas

Citizens of the UK, Ireland, Australia, New Zealand and the EU can enter The Gambia without a visa for trips of under 90 days, provided they have a full passport with at least six months to run from their date of return.

US and Canadian citizens require a visa that should be obtained before travel from the Embassy of The Gambia.

Cards and traveller's cheques

Credit and debit cards are not widely used. Most restaurants and shops operate on a cash-only basis except in the large hotels and for booking tours. There are ATMs on the Senegambia Strip, on Nelson Mandela Street in Banjul and at the Standard Chartered Bank on Kairaba Avenue, all of which are usually empty. You can exchange cash and traveller's cheques at hotels, banks and bureaux de change in the tourist areas. Cash is easier to exchange and you'll get a better rate than for traveller's cheques; however, if you lose your cheques or have them stolen, you can get replacements.

Upcountry, exchange opportunities are scarce, so it is wise to carry enough dalasis (*see p142*) for your needs.

Customs

The following items can be carried into The Gambia without incurring duty.

- 200 cigarettes or 50 cigars or 150g of tobacco
- 1 litre of spirits
- 1 litre of wine or beer
- Goods to the value of D1,000

Electricity

The Gambia operates on a 220V AC system. Electric sockets are a mixture of European-style 2-pin and UK-style 3-pin varieties. Electricity supplies are poor and overstretched and you will encounter regular power cuts. It might be practical to pack a torch or some candles and matches.

Email and Internet

You'll find Internet cafés with cheap access in all towns. Some hotels will have guest Internet access (at extra cost).

Green tourist taxis on the Senegambia Strip

Language

Each of the ethnic groups in The Gambia has its own language, but Gambians also speak the main language of the region if they are born into a minor ethnic group. The main language of the Kombos is Wolof, while upcountry it's Mandinka.

However, the second/third language of every Gambian and the official language of government and the media is English. In the Kombos and tourist areas you'll have no problem making yourself understood if you are an English-speaker.

Media

The press in The Gambia is under pressure to keep a pro-government line, and the murder in 2004 of Deyda Hydara, a leading journalist opposed to President Jammeh, raised the stakes, though journalists do try to instigate political debate and discussion. Printed in English, the papers include *The Point* (*http://thepoint.gm*), where Hydara worked, *The Gambia Daily*, *The Daily Observer* and left-wing *Foroyaa*.

Gambia Television has only been broadcasting since 1995 and there is little home-produced programming, but the TV news also takes a predominantly pro-government line.

Money

The currency of The Gambia is the dalasi, signified by the letter D or GMD. Dalasi notes come in denominations of 5, 10, 25, 50 and 100 and there are 1 dalasi coins. Each dalasi is made up of 100 bututs, and the 50 butut coin is the most common. Most other butut coins are no longer used.

In December 2015 The Gambia is due to join the West Africa Monetary Zone, along with Ghana, Guinea, Nigeria and Sierra Leone, and a new currency, the eco, will be introduced to replace the dalasi.

Opening hours

Shops: Monday–Thursday 8am–7pm, Friday & Saturday 8am–noon, with markets open Monday–Saturday all day. Government offices: Monday–Thursday 8am–4pm, Saturday 8am–noon. Tourist restaurants: 8am–midnight if they serve breakfast, otherwise they open around 11am. Banks: Monday–Thursday 8am–1pm & 4–6pm, Friday 8–11am.

Photographing birds by the stream in Kotu

Post offices: Monday–Thursday
8.20am–12.15pm & 2–4pm, Friday &
Saturday 8.30am–12.15pm.

Pharmacies

Pharmacies are not widespread in The
Gambia but doctors can also supply
drugs and treatments. If you need
prescription medicines, you should bring
enough for your needs during your stay.
If you do need a pharmacy during your
stay in The Gambia, your hotel reception
or tour rep should be able to help.

Post

The postal service in The Gambia is
incredibly slow and you'll often arrive
back home well before any postcards
you may have sent. The main
Government Post Office (GPO) is on
Russell Street in Banjul, close to
Albert Market.

Public holidays
Fixed dates
1 January New Year's Day
18 February Independence Day
1 May Labour Day
22 July Revolution Day
15 August Assumption Day
25 December Christmas Day

Moveable dates
Easter Sunday and Easter Monday
Milad al-Nabi: the Prophet
Muhammad's birthday
Koriteh: the feast that marks the end
of Ramadan
Tobaski: the feast of the sacrifice,
coinciding with the Hajj pilgrimage
to Mecca

Most businesses are also closed on
the last Saturday of every month for
Clean the Nation Day, when local
groups are organised to clean a
communal area of litter.

Suggested reading
The following titles are recommended
to help you understand the background
to the development of The Gambia as a
political entity and a multifaceted
society. There are also books to help
you identify the animals and birds you
spot when there.

Birds of The Gambia and Senegal
Clive Barlow (Christopher Helm
Publishers). The birdwatchers' 'bible',
with pages of pictures, and field notes
on habits and diet.

Common Reptiles of The Gambia,
Common Mammals of The Gambia
and *Common Amphibians of The
Gambia* Linda Barnett and Craig
Emms (Darwin Field Station for
Biodiversity Research; *see p44*). These
three booklet guides, aimed at the
interested amateur, have useful
information with excellent photography
that will help you identify animals you
come across on your travels.

Roots: The Saga of an American Family
Alex Haley (Vintage). The story of
Haley's family tree, traced from Kunta
Kinte of Juffureh, taken into slavery
and sold in America, through the
generations to author Alex Haley
(*see pp76–7*).

CONVERSION TABLE

FROM	TO	MULTIPLY BY
Inches	Centimetres	2.54
Feet	Metres	0.3048
Yards	Metres	0.9144
Miles	Kilometres	1.6093
Acres	Hectares	0.4047
Gallons	Litres	4.5461
Ounces	Grams	28.35
Pounds	Grams	453.6
Pounds	Kilograms	0.4536
Tons	Tonnes	1.016

To convert back, for example from centimetres to inches, divide by the number in the third column.

The Rough Guide to World Music: Africa and the Middle East Simon Broughton et al. (Rough Guides). A detailed explanation and discussion of West African music and its influence on modern 'world music'.

Historical Dictionary of The Gambia Arnold Hughes and Harry Gailey (Scarecrow Press). Hughes was director of the Centre of West African Studies and Gailey is professor of African Studies at San José University. Both are eminently qualified to lead the reader through the intricacies of the history of The Gambia.

Griot and Griottes: Masters of Words and Music Thomas A. Hale (Indiana University Press). A fascinating book about the role of musicians and storytellers in West African society.

Telephones

Telecommunications are provided in the main by Gamtel. Most hotels provide international direct dialling but mark-ups are high. The alternatives are to buy a calling card from Gamtel offices (there is one in every town), or make a call from a Gamtel office and pay at the end of your call. Mobile provision is good along the coastal strip and Gamtel; Africell, Comium and Qcell have connections with the major call companies (check with your provider before leaving home). Roaming charges are high and it may be more cost-effective to buy a Gambian SIM card at a Gamtel office and use that during your stay.

The international code for The Gambia is 220 followed by a seven-figure number.

Time

The Gambia operates in the same time zone as Greenwich Mean Time, which means noon in Banjul is noon in London (October–March), 7am in New York and Toronto, 10pm in Sydney and midnight in Wellington.

Toilets

Public toilets are non-existent in The Gambia. You'll need to visit facilities in cafés, tourist attractions and hotels. Toilets in international establishments should be European style. At local cafés, toilet rolls may not be available, so always carry some just in case.

When travelling upcountry and in the national parks there are no public

Horse riding along Kotu beach at sunset

toilets. In an emergency you'll need to take refuge behind a verdant bush – but check for snakes first.

Travellers with disabilities

There is scant provision for people with disabilities in The Gambia. Some hotels are built on a single storey but few have rooms designed specifically for disabled travellers. Getting around isn't easy on dirt tracks and uneven pavements;

however, there will always be someone willing to help in difficult situations. There is no adapted public transport and disabled visitors should get the advice of a travel agent or tour operator before booking.

For more holiday and travel information for people with disabilities contact:
Holiday Care Services.
Tel: 0845 124 9971 (UK).
www.tourismforall.org.uk

Emergencies

Emergency numbers
Ambulance *16*
Police *17*
Fire Service *18*

Health risks
If you intend to spend most of your time on the beach and around the pool, you won't need vaccinations. If you are planning to spend any time upcountry or travel long distances on public transport, however, then it would be wise to plan a vaccination programme with your doctor. Ensure that your meningitis, polio, yellow fever, typhoid, tetanus and hepatitis A needs are discussed. It's important to state that the risk of these diseases throughout The Gambia is low, but it's better to be safe.

A much more potent risk in The Gambia, however, is malaria, a potentially fatal disease carried by mosquitoes. The disease is passed to humans through the bite of an infected insect, and the most effective way to reduce risk is not to get bitten in the first place. Cover up exposed skin, especially around sunset and through the night, use insect spray or cream on your skin and put insecticide in your room (either spray or light a coil). If mosquitoes are present in the bedroom, sleep under a mosquito net.

Anti-malaria medication offers protection against the disease. This comes in several types, each with a particular regime and some possible side effects, so getting advice from your doctor is of paramount importance. Take the tablets as instructed to ensure maximum protection.

No course of prophylactic tablets is 100 per cent effective, so it is important that, if you have flu-like symptoms any time up to a year after returning from The Gambia, you visit your doctor and have a blood test to rule out malaria as the cause.

Most travellers find that an upset stomach is the worst they suffer while in The Gambia. This can easily be caused by a change in diet or too much sun and usually improves with a day of no solid food and plenty of fluids.

Healthcare
Healthcare provision is not widespread in The Gambia; the system is underfunded and lacks much of the specialist equipment found in hospitals in Europe and North America.

The main hospital is the **Royal Victoria Teaching Hospital** (*tel: 422 8223*) on Independence Drive in Banjul, and there is a new hospital at Farafenni. Smaller towns have local clinics, but these have few resources.

Private clinics in the tourist area include the **Lamtoro Clinic** (*tel: 446 0934*) on the Senegambia Strip, and the

Westfield Clinic (*tel: 439 2213*), on Westfields Road, Serrekunda.

Carrying a small collection of basic medicines such as paracetamol/aspirin and anti-diarrhoea tablets should see you through most health problems.

Insurance

Having adequate insurance cover is vital. The Gambia has no reciprocal health agreements with other countries and visitors will have to pay for any treatment they need. Travellers should ensure that they have cover for private treatment of illness or injury and cover for repatriation back home.

Travellers should always have cover for everything they carry with them in case of loss or theft.

Insurance companies also usually provide cover for cancellation or travel delay in their policies. Though not essential cover, this offers some compensation if travel plans go awry.

Crime and scams

Petty crime such as theft is a growing problem in the tourist area. Don't carry large amounts of cash or flaunt expensive items. Keep money etc. in a secure interior pocket and lock valuables in the hotel safe.

Begging and 'bumstering' (*see pp16–17*) are an irritation more than a danger, and the amounts of money requested are generally small.

Be warned that homosexuality is illegal under The Gambian Criminal Code, and that the police are actively enforcing this code. Transgression could result in up to 14 years in prison.

Embassies

Australia Australian High Commission, *2 Second Rangoon Close, Accra, Ghana. Tel: (233) 302 216 400.*
www.ghana.embassy.gov.au
Canada The Canadian Embassy, *Rue Gallieni X Amadou Cissé Dia, Dakar, Senegal. Tel: (221) 33 889 4700.*
www.canadainternational.gc.ca
New Zealand High Commission of New Zealand, *125 Middel Street, New Muckleneuk, Pretoria 0028, South Africa. Tel: (27 12) 435 9000.*
www.nzembassy.com
South Africa South African Embassy, *Mermoz Sud, Lotissement Ecole de Police Lot no. 5, Dakar, Senegal. Tel: (221) 33 865 1959. www.saesenegal.info*
UK British High Commission, *48 Atlantic Road, Fajara (PO Box 507), Banjul. Tel: 449 5133.*
http://ukingambia.fco.gov.uk
US Embassy of the United States, *Kairaba Avenue, Fajara (PMB 19), Banjul. Tel: 439 2856.*
http://banjul.usembassy.gov

Police

The police in The Gambia have a reasonable reputation, better than most in Africa. Make sure you carry identification and papers for your vehicle if you are driving. Tourist police patrol the resorts and popular beaches. *Police Headquarters, Ecowas Avenue, Banjul. Tel: 422 7222.*

Directory

Accommodation price ratings

Most hotels in The Gambia price rooms in a major foreign currency, usually either pounds sterling or euros. The price guide here (per room) has taken current pricing and converted it to dalasi (approximately 42 dalasi to the pound sterling), but prices may vary due to fluctuating exchange rates.

The upcountry lodges are priced very differently from hotels along the southwest coast, and most fall into the lowest price bracket.

£	under 1,500 dalasi
££	1,500–3,000 dalasi
£££	3,000–4,000 dalasi
££££	over 4,000 dalasi

Eating out price ratings

There's a big price difference between local eateries and the restaurants that serve the tourist coast, so price ranges here concentrate on helping you decide which are inexpensive or expensive tourist-oriented places to eat.

Prices are for a three-course dinner for one without drinks.

£	under 300 dalasi
££	300–750 dalasi
£££	750–1,000 dalasi
££££	over 1,000 dalasi

BANJUL

ACCOMMODATION

Denton's Beach Resort £

Right on the beach at Denton Bridge with the best range of watersports on the doorstep. The three lodges and four rooms mean it's a cosy place to stay. There's a seafood restaurant on-site but very little else in the immediate vicinity, so you'll need a taxi or car if you want to venture out.
Denton Bridge, Banjul. Tel: 777 3777.

Sitanunku Lodge £££

Located on the North Bank, the new Sitanunku Lodge enjoys a secluded waterfront setting on the peninsula overlooking Dog Island. With 16 comfortable en-suite rooms, the solar-powered lodge is perfect for a more adventurous holiday experience. Dog Island is home to the country's best fishing grounds, but for non-anglers there is a sandy beach nearby, plus a small pool, restaurant and bar.
Dog Island, accessed via boat from Denton Bridge. Book through The Gambia Experience (www.gambia.co.uk) or African Angler (www.african-angling.co.uk).

Laico Atlantic Hotel ££££

The most luxurious hotel in the capital, the Laico Atlantic Hotel is a favourite with business travellers to The Gambia but also has good leisure facilities including a gym, a pool, a spa and a private sandy beach, and the grounds are well

kept. It's just a couple of minutes' walk into the heart of Banjul but nightlife in the capital is limited so not really recommended for night owls.
Mummar El Ghaffi Avenue, Banjul. Tel: 422 8601. www.laicohotels.com

EATING OUT
King of Shawarma £–££
This casual eat-in/take-away restaurant has long been a favourite lunch option for locals and expats who work in the Banjul area. As the name suggests, *shawarmas* are on the menu, as are other simple Lebanese dishes. Also serves freshly made juices.
Nelson Mandela Street, Old Town, Banjul. Tel: 422 9799. Open: Mon–Sat 9am–7pm.
Michel's Seafood Restaurant ££
One of the few formal restaurants in the capital, Michel's draws the expats and civil servants from the government offices. It's a good option if you don't want a simple snack.

29 Independence Drive, Banjul. Tel: 422 3108. Open: Mon–Sat 11am–3pm, 6–9pm.

ENTERTAINMENT
Nightclub
The Laico Atlantic Hotel is one of the few places with activities after dark and attracts tourists, expats and Gambians in the evenings. It's at its busiest at weekends.
Laico Atlantic Hotel, Mummar El Ghaffi Avenue, Banjul. Tel: 422 8601. www.laicohotels.com

SPORT AND LEISURE
Denton Bridge Watersports
Organises deep-sea, sport fishing trips, and rental kayaks and wave runners for inshore exploration.
Denton Bridge, Banjul. Tel: 777 3777.
Gambia Tours
The largest and longest-established ground tour operator in the country. Has a full range of day tours and can book trips around the country.
PO Box 217, Banjul. Tel: 446 2601. www.gambiatours.gm

SERREKUNDA AND THE TOURIST COAST
ACCOMMODATION
Sukuta Camping £
This German-owned campsite is well known by those travelling on the trans-Africa trails, arriving overland from Mauritania to the north or from the centre of the continent. Prices are incredibly inexpensive either for a site or for a bungalow, and there's a restaurant on-site. The owners have lots of experience of independent travelling in Africa and are a mine of good advice.
Bijilo Road, Sukuta. Tel: 991 7786. www.campingsukuta.com
African Village Hotel £–££
This small budget hotel gets lots of repeat visitors for its location close to Cape Point and its good food. The rooms are designed like African round huts – hence the hotel name – and are basic but clean, and there's a pool and beach access. It could do with a bit of sprucing up though.

98 Atlantic Road, Bakau.
Tel: 449 5384.

Palm Beach Hotel ££
The rooms of the Palm Beach are spacious and clean, though some of the fittings are a little worn. The hotel sits on a wonderful stretch of beach, with sunbeds sheltered by mature palms. Blocks of rooms are divided by narrow alleys bedecked with flowers and trees, which can make the lower rooms quite dark.
Ask for an upper room or a room facing out of the resort if you'd prefer more light.
Each room has a small balcony or patio and the hotel has a reasonable-sized pool and a restaurant.
Off Kotu Stream Road,
Kotu. Tel: 446 2111.
www.palmbeachhotel.gm

Safari Garden Hotel ££
Excellent, small, Gambian-owned hotel with pretty, bright rooms, each with a spacious patio, and there's a small communal pool set in a private courtyard. There's a restaurant on-site and

activities such as batik, yoga and drumming. The hotel is a member of the Association of Small-Scale Enterprises in Tourism and is keen to encourage fair trade and sustainability.
Off Atlantic Road, Fajara.
Tel: 449 5887.
www.safarigarden.com

Bakotu Hotel £££
Set on the landward side of Kotu Stream Road, the lack of direct access to the beach is the only disadvantage of this well-designed resort, with The Captain's Table gourmet restaurant on-site (*see pp152–3*). Rooms are well furnished for the price, and there's a small pool area and guest laundry facilities. Some rooms overlook the stream with its wealth of birdlife. It's only a couple of minutes to a range of restaurants and to Kotu beach itself.
2 Kotu Stream Road,
Kotu. Tel: 446 5555.
www.bakotuhotel.com

Omakan Hotel £££
A lodge hotel opened in late 2006, the Omakan is a Gambian-owned and European-managed

boutique property, fitted and decorated to a high standard. Accommodation is made up of good-sized rooms and spacious bungalows set around a pretty plunge pool. There's a nice bar and a good restaurant on-site (food can be served in your suite or bungalow). It's quiet and secluded for those who want a personal retreat.
Sukuta Village.
Tel: 768 3672.
www.omakanhotel.com

Senegambia Beach Hotel £££
The largest hotel in The Gambia has been a long-standing favourite for many years and continues to impress with a good standard of accommodation and communal space – even if some of the design elements look a little bit dated. The gardens are spacious, and there are two pools, tennis courts and a spa, plus the restaurants and bars of the Senegambia Strip just outside the door. There's even a resident bird

specialist who'll give you a tour of the grounds. *Senegambia Road, Kololi. Tel: 466 2717. www. senegambiahotel.com*

Sunbeach Hotel £££

A pretty, low-rise resort of 184 rooms and suites right at the tip of Cape Point, with spacious accommodation, generous patios and garden areas, some with sea views. The furniture is bright, with colourful fabrics mixed with rattan and bamboo. The hotel features two restaurants, including a buffet venue and a pizza parlour, and has a good-sized pool, so it's a great family option. The beach here curves around the point, offering a picturesque vista. *Kofi Annan Street, Cape Point, Bakau. Tel: 449 7190. www.sunbeachhotel.com*

Coconut Residence ££££

A beautifully designed and furnished tropical lodge, Coconut Residence sets itself apart from others in its class with luxurious modern touches and a sophisticated ambience. The rooms can't be faulted and there's a gourmet restaurant, plunge pool and lush landscaped gardens. Perhaps the only disadvantage is that it doesn't have beach access, and the atmosphere favours adults rather than families. *Kerr Serign, Serrekunda. Tel: 446 3377. www. coconutresidence.com*

Coco Ocean Resort and Spa ££££

Luxurious and opulent beachfront resort with a health and beauty spa, gym, three restaurants and a bar. There are 24 suites and penthouses, some with a private pool. Same owners as the Coconut Residence. *1 Bamboo Drive, Kombo Coastal Highway, Bijilo. Tel: 446 6500. www.cocoocean.com*

Kairaba Beach Hotel ££££

A sympathetically designed four-star hotel set at the beach end of the Senegambia Strip, the Kairaba has spacious and elegantly designed tropical rooms set in verdant gardens and fronting onto a large, free-form pool. Standard rooms are set on the land-side of the reception area opposite the hotel offices, so their location isn't as good as more de-luxe room options. *Senegambia Road, Kololi. Tel: 446 2940. www.kairabahotel.com*

Mandina Lodge ££££

Award-winning eco-lodge with luxury rooms floating on the *bolong* or surrounded by the jungle. The Lodge has less than a dozen detached suites, some floating on the water of Mandina Bolong, others set in the sacred forest itself. This is a place to seriously chill out rather than for those wanting a fast-paced beach break. *Makasutu Culture Forest, Mandina Ba. Tel: 990 0268. www.makasutu.com*

Ngala Lodge ££££

This small European-owned lodge has grown out of the ruin of an old ambassador's mansion. Ngala has a range of individually furnished rooms, from boutique-style suites to luxury

African bungalows, all set in verdant tropical gardens and overlooking the ocean. The restaurant is excellent (*see p153*).
64 Atlantic Boulevard, Fajara. Tel: 449 4045.
www.ngalalodge.com
(packages booked through The Gambia Experience; www.gambia.co.uk).

Ocean Bay ££££
A well-designed addition on Cape Point, the low-rise Ocean Bay features spacious rooms with well-proportioned dark wood furnishings and good-sized patio or balcony. There are several restaurants on-site, a pool, children's pool and a range of sports. There's also a children's club.
Kofi Annan Street, Cape Point, Bakau.
Tel: 449 4265.
www.oceanbayhotel.com

Sandele Bay Eco-Retreat ££££
Opened in late 2007 by the owners of the Safari Garden Hotel and situated about 100m (110yds) from the beach, this is a sustainable and eco-friendly construction, with a good restaurant on-site.

Kartong. Tel: 449 5887.
www.sandele.com

Sheraton Gambia Hotel, Resort and Spa ££££
This beautifully-styled African adobe resort is the first luxury spa hotel in The Gambia. The whole resort is exquisitely designed with modern African-Asian furnishings and design elements set in adobe-style, mud-walled, low-rise buildings.
The 195 rooms are cool and elegant in neutral tones embellished by the warmth of hardwood accents. There is an all-day dining restaurant and a fusion evening-only dining option.
Brufut Heights,
AU Highway, Serrekunda.
Tel: 441 0889.
www.starwoodhotels.com

EATING OUT

Boss Lady ££
A great African restaurant where you can try Gambian staples including *domoda*, *benachin* and *yassa*. No alcohol.
Kotu Beach. No phone.
Open: daily 5–11pm.

Solomon's ££
The best place for fish and chips in The Gambia – served in foil, right on the beach. Order ahead though, as it can take some time.
Palma Rima Road, Kololi. Tel: 439 6490.
Open: daily.

Al Basha Lebanese Restaurant £££
Excellent Lebanese *mezze* (collection of small dishes that make up a full meal) and grilled meats. The décor will certainly get you in the mood for Eastern promise.
Senegambia Road, Kololi. Tel: 446 3300. Open: daily 7pm–midnight.

The Captain's Table £££
The menu at this gourmet restaurant changes with the seasons, as only local organic ingredients make the grade, but meat always includes the excellent local Ndama beef fillet. A range of international dishes mixes with Asian and Arab suggestions. The restaurant is nicely designed and service is attentive.
2 Kotu Stream Road, Kotu. Tel: 446 5555.

www.bakotuhotel.com.
Open: daily noon–11pm.

**The Green Mamba
Garden £££**

Mongolian grill-style
buffet restaurant and bar
with pool tables, great
atmosphere and music.
A favourite of the expats,
it has weekly new movie
nights and draught
JulBrew. Try one of the
many unique cocktails
infused with local juices.
Senegambia Road, Kololi.
Tel: 656 2622. www.
greenmambagarden.com.
Open: daily 6pm–late.

**The Kora Bar and
Restaurant £££**

Beautifully-built
restaurant on the more
serene side of the tourist
strip, with a luscious
garden, and great food
and service. Try the
chicken fajitas, seafood
feast for two or the
grilled fillet steak. Also,
the freshly made
profiteroles and
cheesecakes are a must
for dessert. As well as
being a great restaurant,
The Kora turns into
the place to be as an
excellent bar for cocktails
in the late evenings, with
a fresh mix of music and

entertainment. Very
popular with locals
and expats.
Senegambia Road, Kololi.
Tel: 446 2727. www.
thekorarestaurant.com.
Open: daily 6pm–late.

**The Butcher's
Shop ££££**

Every expat knows where
The Butcher's Shop is –
it's been supplying
excellent free-range meat
since 1993, and has
expanded into a
delicatessen. Only later
did the owners develop
the restaurant, but it's
now one of the best
eateries in the country,
if a little run-down.
Breakfast and lunches see
excellent pastries,
sandwiches and fresh
fruit juices. Sumptuous
meat dishes pad out
salads and Mediterranean
dishes at dinner. It's
expensive, but excellent.
130 Kairaba Avenue,
Fajara. Tel: 449 5069.
Open: Mon–Sat
8am–late.

Ngala Lodge ££££

If you don't stay at the
Ngala Lodge, it's worth
booking a table at the
restaurant and dressing
up for the best European

food in The Gambia.
There's live music in the
background and a decent
wine list. Worth pushing
the boat out for.
64 Atlantic Boulevard,
Bakau. Tel: 449 7672.
www.ngalalodge.com.
Open: Mon–Sat 7–10pm.

Shikra ££££

The Kairaba Hotel's
fine-dining option is a
beautifully designed Asian
restaurant concentrating
on Thai dishes but with
delicate sushi and some
Chinese options. There's
also a choice of vegetarian
offerings.
Kairaba Hotel,
Senegambia Road, Kololi.
Tel: 446 2940.
www.kairabahotel.com.
Open: Mon–Sat 7–11pm.

ENTERTAINMENT

Aquarius Café

One of the lounge/clubs
that offers a different
style of music each
night. There's always a
good crowd during the
tourist season.
Senegambia Road, Kololi.
Tel: 446 0247.
Open: daily 6pm–5am.

Churchill's

A long-standing
favourite British-owned

bar that has popular karaoke evenings and live Premiership matches for football fans. Be aware though that it has something of a reputation as a gathering place for prostitutes.
Palma Rima Road, Kotu. Tel: 990 3383. Open: daily 11am–1am.

Jokor

The most famous *mbalax* club in The Gambia, Jokor throbs with great music at weekends and hosts fantastic live concerts. During the week there's a different sound every evening. It's a great place to meet locals, although use caution as tourists have sometimes been robbed or harassed.
Westfield Junction, Serrekunda. Tel: 437 5690. Open: daily midnight–5am.

Paparazzi

A small and popular bar on the Senegambia tourist strip that gets crowded quickly with locals, tourists and flight crew. Entertaining barmen, good strong cocktails, a propensity for House music, and a

cool VIP lounge out back if you want to indulge yourself.
Senegambia Road, Kololi. Tel: 446 0600. Open: daily 10pm–5am.

Rainbow Beach Bar

Large and pleasant beach bar with good food, including local dishes, fish and chips, and even tandoori chicken. There is simple accommodation at the back.
Sanyang. Open: daily.

Seaview Beach Bar

A great terrace with views over the beach, this is a good vantage point for a sunset drink or later when there is live entertainment.
Off Bertil Harding Highway near the Senegambia Hotel, Kololi. Tel: 446 3502. Open: daily 11am–2am.

Wow Nightclub

Small joint playing a mixture of disco, reggae and rap. It's popular with tourists and locals, although beware of the bumsters.
Senegambia Road, Kololi. Tel: 446 6186. Open: daily 10pm–5am.

SPORT AND LEISURE

Bijilo Forest Park

Often referred to as 'The Monkey Park', this small wildlife reserve features a well-maintained series of marked trails through dense, shady vegetation, with glimpses of the blue Atlantic waters and golden beaches along one side of the perimeter. Both the green vervet (callithrix) and red colobus monkeys are found in abundance in the park, as are numerous species of bird. It is but a remnant of what most of the Gambian coast used to look like.
Near the end of the main tourist strip in Senegambia. Open: daily. Admission charge.

Bird Guide Association

This bona fide organisation has a hut next to Kotu Stream and you can contract a guide to show you the best spots in the area.
Kotu Bridge, Kotu Stream Road, Kotu. Tel: 998 2234.

Camel Safari

Treks down Tanje beach on the back of a dromedary.

Coast Road, Tanje Village.
Tel: 446 1083.

Darboes Bicycle Hire/Rental Service

Bicycle rental by the hour or the day.

Kotu Stream Road, Kotu (opposite the Badala Hotel).
Tel: 770 1587.

Fajara Country Club

Has The Gambia's best golf course (over 16s only), and facilities for a range of other sports.
Atlantic Road, Fajara.
Tel: 449 5457.

Gambian Reptiles Farm

Owned by a Frenchman, Mr Luc Paziaud, and aimed at locals and tourists alike. The owner is trying to prevent certain species from becoming extinct and attempting to educate people on how to deal with reptiles, namely snakes, by teaching locals which ones are venomous. You can spend a good hour or so at the farm with an informative guide, getting an interesting insight into the wildlife that is found in The Gambia, but seldom seen.

Between Gunjur and Kartong, at the side of the main highway. Tel: 700 4672. Open: daily. Admission charge.

Jane's Boats

Morning and afternoon trips around Tanbi Wetlands and expeditions upriver on neatly-kept double-decker pirogues.
PO Box 4414, Bakau.
Tel: 776 8074.

Quest Quad Trekking

A well-established quad-bike rental company. One-hour to two-day treks are available.
Palma Rima Road, Kololi.
Tel: 446 4146. www.monnowevents.co.uk.
Open: daily.

Vitala Spa

Independent spas operating in three hotels on the tourist strip. You can enjoy massage, aromatherapy and other beauty treatments.
Kairaba Hotel (also at the Ocean Bay Hotel and the Sunbeach Hotel), Senegambia Road, Kololi.
Tel: 446 2940.

SHOPPING

Craft markets or bengdulas are found in

the following locations in the Kombos:

Bakau – opposite the African Village Hotel.

Brikama – opposite the police station.

Cape Point – between the Sun Beach and Ocean Bay Hotels.

Fajara – on the beach opposite Hotel Fajara.

Kololi – at the top of Senegambia Road.

Kotu – between the Kombo Beach and Bungalow Beach Hotels.

Lemonfish Art Gallery

Arts workshop with almost 30 local artists displaying work. Gift shop with other crafts on sale.
Kartong Village.
Tel: 764 3948.
www.lemonfish.gm

Topshop

This gift shop sells the best selection of books and maps along the coast, plus a range of tropical clothing, gifts and handicrafts.
Senegambia Beach Hotel, Senegambia Road, Kololi.
Tel: 446 2717.

JANJANGBUREH AND THE MID-RIVER REGION

ACCOMMODATION

Baobolong Camp £

A cluster of round huts set around a communal courtyard, this is a basic but clean option with friendly staff. Several suites have been added facing the river.
Owen Street, Janjangbureh. Tel: 567 6133.

Bird Safari Camp £

Set on the water's edge, accommodation is a mixture of 'Out of Africa' safari tents and round huts, and it's surrounded by riverine forest.
1.5km (1 mile) north of Janjangbureh, McCarthy Island. Tel: 733 6570 (office in Janjangbureh). www.bsc.gm

Janjangbureh Camp £

Set on the riverbank north of the island, Janjangbureh Camp has nicely-designed, rustic rooms and a good restaurant serving Gambian dishes. There's no electricity, so it's very peaceful and the property is lit at night by romantic kerosene lamps. There are free boat transfers into town.
North shore, opposite Janjangbureh, McCarthy Island. Tel: 976 6588 (office in Bakau).

Tendaba Camp £

Originally built to cater to hunters, this riverside lodge now attracts wildlife watchers, photographers and twitchers from around the world. It's a great place to pick up a guide, and it runs excursions to Kiang West Wetland Reserve and Bao Bolong National Park. Simple rooms, but there's a restaurant, pool and bar overlooking the river.
Tendaba Village, Kwinella. Tel: 554 1024.

Sindola Safari Lodge ££–£££

The most luxurious upcountry game lodge, with abundant grounds and spacious traditional-style lodges, games room and pool. There are wonderful little touches of Africa, like the giant wooden chess set carved into traditional figures and animals.
Kanilai Village. Tel: 448 3415.

Chimp Rehabilitation Visitor Camp ££££

Wilderness tented camp in the heart of the national park where you can spend time with the project workers of the Chimpanzee Rehabilitation Trust. Full board included in the price.
River Gambia National Park (book accommodation through Hidden Gambia; tel: 0121 228 4100 (UK); www.hiddengambia.com).

EATING OUT

Janjangbureh Camp £

The best food in Janjangbureh, served in a round hut-style restaurant with outside tables on the riverside. It is one of the few places upcountry with a choice of vegetarian dishes. Book ahead if you can, especially if you aren't staying at the lodge. There's a boat transfer from Janjangbureh to the north bank across the river.
North shore, opposite Janjangbureh, McCarthy Island. Tel: 449 4360 (company office

in Bakau). Open: daily
7–9pm (book ahead).
Tendaba Camp £
There's a good range
of Gambian food and
international meals and
snacks at the restaurant
here. Nothing fancy, but
it makes a change to be
able to order something
different from the
standard buffet fare
served in most lodges.
Tendaba Village,
Kwinella. Tel: 554 1024.
Open: daily 7am–10pm.
Sindola Lodge £–££
The best upcountry
option, with excellent
Gambian and
international dishes
served in a rustic, bush-
style building in the midst
of the tropical gardens.
Kanilai. Tel: 448 3415.
Open: daily 8–10am,
11am–3pm, 7–9pm.

ENTERTAINMENT
Riverside bar
The wooden bar on a
jetty over the river
shallows is one of the
prettiest places in The
Gambia to enjoy a cold
JulBrew and listen to the
frogs after dark.
Tendaba Camp, Tendaba
Village, Kwinella.

Tel: 554 1024. Open: daily
5–11pm.
Folkloric show
If the Janjangbureh
camps are full or have
big groups, the owners
will usually arrange
for a dancing and
drumming performance
during the evening.
Enquire whether the
lodge you book will have
entertainment or ring
ahead to Baobolong
Camp, Bird Safari Camp
or Janjangbureh Camp.

SPORT AND LEISURE
Janjangbureh Camp
The camp runs batik
courses (must be pre-
booked) so you can learn
about the techniques
used in wax-resist
dyeing.
North shore, opposite
Janjangbureh, McCarthy
Island. Tel: 449 4360
(company office
in Bakau).
Bird Safari Camp
Offers guided cross-
country and river
birdwatching safaris.
1.5km (1 mile) north of
Janjangbureh, McCarthy
Island. Tel: 733 6570
(office in Janjangbureh).
www.bsc.gm

Tendaba Camp is a
centre of excellence for
birdwatching and has a
pool of guides for you to
hire who are highly
experienced in wildlife
and bird tracking. The
camp also runs regular
boat trips to Kiang West
and Bao Bolong parks.
Tendaba Village,
Kwinella. Tel: 554 1024.
Drumming lessons,
Bird Safari Camp
organises regular
drumming courses for
beginners and improvers
(also Janjangbureh
Camp, details above).
1.5km (1 mile) north of
Janjangbureh, McCarthy
Island. Tel: 733 6570
(office in Janjangbureh).
www.bsc.gm
Kayaking,
Janjangbureh Camp
has kayaks for hire so
that you can explore
the river.
North shore, opposite
Janjangbureh, McCarthy
Island. Tel: 976 6588
(office in Bakau).

SHOPPING
Lumos (country markets)
take place in Farafenni
on Sundays and in Koto
on Mondays.

Index

Acknowledgements

Thomas Cook Publishing wishes to thank PETE BENNETT, to whom the copyright belongs, for the photographs in this book, except for the following images:

LISA VOORMEIJ 1, 5, 17, 41, 56, 71, 115
KIM KOMBO PLANTATION AND DISTILLERY 63
PICTURES COLOUR LIBRARY 75, 111
THOMAS COOK 58 (Paul Walters), 110 (Grant Rooney)
WIKIMEDIA COMMONS 45 (KG), 76

The author and photographer would like to thank Batch S Fye for his logistical help during research for the book and Mandi Watson for her unending enthusiasm, support and friendship.

For CAMBRIDGE PUBLISHING MANAGEMENT LIMITED:
Project editor: Tom Lee
Typesetter: Paul Queripel
Proofreaders: Jan McCann & Ed Robinson
Indexer: Karolin Thomas

SEND YOUR THOUGHTS TO
BOOKS@THOMASCOOK.COM

We're committed to providing the very best up-to-date information in our travel guides and constantly strive to make them as useful as they can be. You can help us to improve future editions by letting us have your feedback. If you've made a wonderful discovery on your travels that we don't already feature, if you'd like to inform us about recent changes to anything that we do include, or if you simply want to let us know your thoughts about this guidebook and how we can make it even better – we'd love to hear from you.

Send us ideas, discoveries and recommendations today and then look out for your valuable input in the next edition of this title.

Emails to the above address, or letters to the traveller guides Series Editor, Thomas Cook Publishing, PO Box 227, Coningsby Road, Peterborough PE3 8SB, UK.

Please don't forget to let us know which title your feedback refers to!